The Guerrilla Employee

Survival and Game Changing Strategies for
Startup Employees

Vindika Lokunarangodage

2019

ISBN 978-955-35840-1-4

Content

Preface

The book is intended for startup employees who just started their carriers in the corporate world. However, it can be used by any employee who is basically in trouble due to their own circumstances. It is not a practical guide book or manual, but some commonsense thoughts which are written in an easy to understand manner with reference to practical experiences. The key elements of the book is to understand the work environment while responding according to the existing situation for the survival within the organization.

The book is trying to address the internal demotivation and frustrations faced by new employees at their startup career through short answers within; instead of moving around while creating some stable footage to hold the ground. Thus, offering options of survival according to the situations rather than focusing on the rivals. Hence, explained methods or tactics may be controversial, non like standard practices. However, the use and the application of such activities solely on the reader where his choices should be based on the knowledge and experience, but not anxiety or fear.

Vindika Lokunarangodage

February, 2019

Acknowledgements

Author gratefully acknowledge the dedicated support of previous employers who has help understand the corporate world in a different perspective.

The subordinates work under the author in many organizations and specially the Gen Z, trainees who were a great influence to understand the changing dynamics of startups in modern work environment.

Author highly indebted to Artist Priyantha Abeysundara for his invaluable time and hand for the artworks as well as the amazing graphics by Hasantha Wijethunga.

Friends and family, society and technology that helps converting these gross ideas into a manuscript.

Guerrilla:

One who engages in irregular warfare especially as a member of an independent unit.

- Webster's New Collage Dictionary, 2008.

Rather than acting openly, guerrillas often choose to remain "in the closet," moving clandestinely behind the scenes, salmon swimming upstream against the current of power.

Guerrilla runs the spectrum from anti-establishment liberals to fundamentalist conservatives, from constructive contributors to deviant destroyers.

- Rosemary O'Leary, 2010.

Market Trends in Corporate World

Today, the jobs are different, achievements are different and people are different. Thus, it is always challenging to become a successful employee in any organization, because there are many pitfalls even before you start your first job. On the other hand, being a successful employee doesn't always mean that you are an honored/excellent employee. Consider few decades before, date back to 1970s to 1990s, the age millennial or even before them the baby boomers, if you asked from someone "what is their job", most people happy to say that they are working for some big corporation or a multinational and society accepted it where everyone wanted to work for a such company may be like Coca Cola, 3M, AT&T, IBM, Toyota, Nestle, GM, Ford or even some unknown local giant. But if you ask the same question from a young employee in current society, the **Gen Z** or iGen or plurals as many explained them; he/she will love to say that she/he is a software engineer or may be a consultant or even some kind of a technical expert.

In fact, I recently interviewed a young undergraduate for an in-plant training where I asked what is her future objective, may be if I was asked the same question over decade ago when I was searching for a training assignment; my most probable answer would have been to join the company and become an executive manager there. But do you think her answer was same like mine ten years back; of course not, she said she want to be a consultant. That's because employees in current society no more value about being some company's long-term prisoner and they want to jump the band wagon to become experts or professionals of the field they work in the market.

That's because the giant or small companies are not so important in the current market where people look into the opportunities while improving their paycheck as well as the working conditions coupled with various achievements. On the other hand, employers are also tricky and tactical none like old days where they use various tactics to control employees through labour laws as well as many different illegal practices or loopholes in the law to maximize their profits.

One of such examples is that, when you were interviewed and bargained for a job and the moment company understands that you are the right choice. They will tell you that, we still only see your CV and we just heard of your talks but we need to see how you practically good before you get your full benefits; you may have nothing to bargain any further, if you like the job or if it is the breakthrough you wanted; you will definitely accept the job thinking that they will provide you all the benefits or promises as agreed. Now you are optimistic about the situation, there is nothing wrong about it, but the tricky employer always know that you can't be accurate always as you promised, hence you will make some mistakes.

Make an entrance - Make a difference

Then you join the company and start to work as well as determined to work hard, but eventually you will make some mistakes, employer noticed it. However, it goes unnoticed may be around 8 to 9 months most possibly, but all of a sudden some warning latter appear in your personnel file pinpointing some of the early mistakes as well as some of the new mistakes you did while on duty. It is human nature that no one is perfect, where people tend to do mistakes by mistake. Nevertheless, later may be your boss will see you and talk to you regarding your mistakes while suggesting some remedies for you. Notably. he even may suggest some training programs which you had participated two three years back and he was sorry about you; and want to make you a better employee.

Eventually, you accept all that and you even will participate in the training program that he proposed from the company training budget. Now I know you will think your boss is very good person and you thank him so much and again start working more motivated than ever. Finally, yearend comes as usual and you are getting the same paycheck as you had in the first month and there is no pay hicks as he promised to upgrade after a year, where you were little upset about it and may be discuss the matter with your family or with your friends at work or outside.

Without a doubt, everyone will propose you to meet your boss and request him to make some arrangements as he promised. But when you meet him, he will be very sorry about the situation and will say that "son I'm really worried about you and I really wanted to increase your salary, unfortunately we have little problems in your personnel file. Since there is a letter about some mistakes you made or performance evaluations are not up to the standard where it is impossible to provide you the promised benefits but if you get improved within the year you will get them by the next year". Certainly, you have no words since his calm and quit gentlemen manner which impressed you as well as his deep worry about your case, where you leave his office mostly disappointed and still blaming yourself about your own mistakes.

Now you may be embarrassed and loss your appetite for work or you will try to improve yourself to get more benefits in the next year. Do you think that he decided to give you the benefits by next year, Hell No! He decided to keep you in the same wage after the first year by the date he recruited you. He make your pitfalls concisely planning it to make you happy and stay while adhering to the same benefits because he want to maximize his profits and want to pay less to achieve that. He is much cunning and tactical than you where he got the advantage of cheating your conscience. If you talk to your friends in the company probably you will find some other guys who also got the same problem once in a while and may be 2 to 3 years later you will get a considerable salary increase or probably allowance to retain you there. But your employer already earned his profit of hiring you within the first year and if he keeps you in the same salary for next year, he further multiply his profits, by paying you less than your real value.

Thus, it is very critical today to bargain before you join for full benefits, later-on you can make some improvements if possible, but there are other ways to handle your employer to bring him to the bargaining table. The best mode is however to jump ship on time, where you should not work more than two years for any employer who do not significantly benefit you within that time period. As a rule of thumb, most of the jump ship employees are successful in one way or the other because they learn lot from the places they passed by and gather different kinds of experiences from the people they work with. On the other hand, they are the most sellable employees in the market. They value themselves and add value to the job they do too.

However, getting up in the management ladder of corporate world is not so easy today, because there is an intense competition among each other and everyone wants to jump into the driving sheet. But it is always a cold war among the existing staff, if the company is not in a position to hire someone outside the company to improve and blend the existing brains with a new brain. Thus, people tend to wash dirty linen in-front of the employer or try to impress him with notorious stories or nonsense to full-down some one really suitable because of the various fringe benefits.

To become a successful employee in current society you need different tools and tactics with long term plans, short term goals and short term plans with long term goals. I know you are little confused about the way I wrote it, but it is the truth; in your employment carrier you need to align your long term plans with short term goals, because you never know the opportunity or the fait until it reaches you. For an example; if you want to be a marketing manager by four years later and if you are just a starter, your short term goals must be to learn the job as quickly as possible while getting some sales. Then you may start taking some classes after you grab some experience to upgrade your theoretical knowledge and paper qualifications. But most importantly you need to start with some small goals focusing the big picture.

In current society, there are two kinds of jobs; one is in government sector while other is private sector. There are many other sub categories that you may came across such as semi government, NGOs and many more. But as a norm, most of the people who works for the government bears a narrow minded future with safety at first. In contrast, private sector people are more resilient and don't much worried about the safety while they are more active in job roles.

> ## Think before Act, Think before Talk

As such, government sector non-incentivized as they get their usual slow growing salary with limited perks and highest job security where they are basically come to spend the day and do whatever they are given. This is one of the major reasons for corruption in the government employments around the world. However, private sector has many incentives for employees with very low job security and if they do not perform very well they are no longer kept for ornaments.

Hence, this book is written on the different aspects, because there are books for you to learn various skills and standard practices. But there are few books you can find in the bookshelves or on the net which explains about how you play your employer or planning your own future in a highly politicized, favor based or nepotism oriented organization. The strategies are practically proven or personnel experiences of various people's lives. Thus, reading it will tell you how you can devise your own survival over the years while becoming an important figure in any difficult place or position. Understanding the personnel potential and capacity will tell you, whether you need to genuinely present yourself or act like one.

> *Nobody is perfect, No system is perfect & No company is perfect.*

The book is written in the perspective of employee looking at an employer as a culprit, but in reality it is not, because the book is trying to focus from a different angle to the same situation. It is to use the existing situation in to your advantages or adaptability, rather than motivating you to follow standard method which are very good, but too theoretical and sometimes never exists. Because most of the books we read, are considering that the working environment is ideal, plus both employer and the employees are honest. Thus, employee was guided to self-motivate to achieve what will be a fair goal as to the theoretical conditions, which are never existed.

Boss is Boss - He is always Right - He is an Idiot

Do you hear this adage? I bet you did at least 100 times in your life time, because it is world famous term and every continent knows it, that's because all the bosses are idiots. Not really, but there is a truth in it. On the other hand, what you never thought was that using the given term to relax your pressure and improving the calmness of your working condition. Other than the top player who owns the business; there is always a boss on top of you. Thus, it is very rare situation that you work in somewhere without a boss as a startup. Then it is very generic or common that you almost get fired by your boss, or very soon you will get it. If you are a new starter; then you need to know that hiring, firing and buttering; all these are part and parcel of the job description or daily routine things.

Because the amount of firing will be decided by your boss's temper, the state of agitation, market pressures, growth pressures, your mistakes and weaknesses as well as how much his wife or husband humiliated him/her before leave for the job in the morning. These are the facts that you don't care where you try to understand your mistakes, but it is bullshit or even horseshit, because you don't want to do anything to forget about it. If you are trying to understand as it is a mistake, now you are mistaken boy!!, you just try to feel that Boss is boss! He is always right! He is an idiot! in your mind. Then you will feel more comfortable because he is paying you not only to take the work he has assigned to you but he also pays you some amounts to use you as a pressure release valve. Okay let's try a simple story, instead of a formal discussion, do you like it? I can tell you many stories regarding different such conditions I faced but here is a one story.

Alright, this is a true story and it happened to me okay? I was handling a large project some time ago as a project manager for a client. We were hiring lots of foreign installation engineers as well as technicians to the project where there were many onsite issues and problems every day. There was an old engineer from Thailand, who was always with me and he was the chief engineer of the project assigned from the machinery supplier. He was very nice at the beginning and one month later; when his time for return was canceled as work planned was unfinished due to their company's some of the wrong parts. He started firing at me sometimes, but he was not firing at anybody other than me. One day, I asked him "why are you always angry with me and firing me, even though I have always supported you while working even out of my boundaries to help you to complete the work within given timelines".

Then he told me, "you are the only one very close to me and I can't shout at my company even though they have done the mistake or your crew. Nonetheless, I'm home sick also, because there are some family matters which he need to be physically there to sort out, but I can't go back without completing this either. So I'm under pressure and only thing I can do is to release it on you" one way or the other. Therefore, when there is a small mistake from any one, he fires me and release his pressure sometimes. (One such example was I'm too fast when I'm talking whether English or my mother tong, where he can't clearly understand my English.) So he apologized me for using me as a pressure release value. Then I realize that people sometimes shout at us not because we make mistakes, but because we sometimes close to them or else that is the only way they can clear their minds. On the other hand, all the time he shouted me, he used to buy some very tasty food or something in the evening and treat me very well to let down his own guilt while teaching me something new or some of the mechanical theories and acts very nicely.

I hope you may have got the point easily what I meant. That's the concept call firing and buttering, in general this is called "you fire the ass; put some butter layer on it". There are many other examples and occasions that I was fired by various bosses in many places. But all those times, if it is not my mistake; I used say to myself "boss is boss, he is always right and he is an idiot" afterwards, because survival is the most important thing even if you want to move from the job that you are doing right now. So calm down, close your eyes; countdown to 100 or even to thousand until you are calmed. Wait till at least until you find your next opportunity, don't run away.

*T*he general meaning of CHANGE is a
movement out of existing state through
transition state to impending state where whole
new circumstances or some makeshift to the
current state will take place. The fundamental
nature of change is that it is the only stable thing
in the world which will come out in various forms
until it converts to something else. Thus, it can

Bend the Rules

---

happen due to the internal or external motivational factors.

Change theory can be defined as all building blocks required for generating a given long-term goal where the set of connected building blocks (interchangeably referred to as outcomes, results, accomplishments, or preconditions) is depicted on a map known as a pathway of change/change framework, which is a graphic representation of the change process whereas change management is the application of a structured process and set of tools for leading the people side of change to achieve a desired outcome.

Oh, Bullshit...........What's this all means????

Okay, let's forget the silly scientific way of talking, I knew you hate me of that,....

So let's go for another story, Have you ever felt that no matter what you do to resolve problems at your work place, you always wind up with more problems each day"? And some days more than others it is practically unbearable, so you feel like running away? If so, do not run because it's not you who should run.

...For an example let's talk about John who wants to change the existing system of a company to build up a new system that could easily increase the efficiency. In order to do that he implements new techniques. As we all know primates, which includes humans by nature have "Neophobia – fear of anything new". Thus, mostly in the beginning, others might not like the idea of being interfered with their routine work. This could cause difficulties for John throughout his journey of "making a change for greater good." As others might disapprove his work and try to bury him because they do not like him messing with their work. So every day John will have to work his best to implement new system as well as to tackle these problems which arise from his co-workers. If he has just aligned with the existing system from the beginning, even though it is old and inefficient, he never would have get into so much trouble...

> ## More work more problems- No work no problems

Are you one of those people who has their names written in big letters in the company's "Most Hated List"? Do your friend count drops down drastically and your enemy count skyrocket every day? Don't worry, as this clearly describes *that you are not a typical employee who just sit idly; but an exceptional employee who wants to tryout something new and different to achieve much more than your salary.*

A frog living in a well can only see the part of the sky framed by the mouth of the well. It does not have any idea about the outer world. So it is really hard to show it that there is whole new world out there and that in order to see outside it must try to escape. Likewise short-sighted and narrow-minded people are the hardest to transform, because in general people hate change.

So the next time if somebody tries to buckle you down, consider it as a good sign. If people are talking about you that means you are noticed. So think the backstabs, sneers are as compliments and carry on your work with more determination hoping that someday the "frogs" will take your advice and jump out.

Follow in Order to Lead

$\mathcal{H}$ay, "war is young men dyeing; old man talking where you need to ignore the politics". Do you know that kings were remembered for the victories of wars, but solders were died who never remembers except for very few occasions? On the other hand if you want to become a king someday you still need to learn to become a king someday.

However, if you want to learn, keep your cup always empty which can be poured, but if your cup is filled already, unfortunately you will not learn anything in life. Always empty cups can be filled without any overflows non like the filled cups, where mentors may like to fill something to your cup, if they noticed that of your cup has some empty space. Nevertheless, always be careful of what you filled with your cup which needs more conscience to be selective. In life, you need to be selective about everything, while choosing a job to a partner to knowledge to anything came across.

I wanna tell you another story, we love stories from the childhood, sometimes it's your mother, sometimes its grandma or grandfather; but rarely your father, that's because he is busy pooling resources for your education or stomach, otherwise you are not there to read these stories. Anyway do you ever heard of the story of the tea cup? Probably not, this is another unheard story again. I love to make things very simple because you will easily read it and remember it. If there's something important; that is what you will use sometimes in case required.

> **Have a notebook & pen in your pocket always –**
> **Jot down everything important**

Okay the moral of the story is about the training of your skills set and about how hard it is, when it comes to corporate world. Corporate world is a place that where free market is floating around you and you will become a fine figure with many talents or no talents of any kind. Do you know what f-i-n-e stand for; its freaky, ironic, nauseous and emotional, okay I'm kidding you.

Let's talk about training of your first job, of-cause you need some training before you start. Each new job you take in first time; you need some guidance but if there is no one to let you know what to do, then you may end up with nowhere at the end of the day or you will be a strategic person who may find out some luck or way out by cross reference to your previous encounters of life.

It is very important to manage your works on time with high accuracy which is not so easy as a matter of fact, because if you don't have a mentor or supervisor you are just like a boat without a sail. Do you know when and where you are going to get some storms or calm waters for the ride? If you had a captain in your boat he may let you know how to make a sail or how to use a wooden stick as a paddle at least which he could find to get you to the water and to take you down the river without hitting on the rocks down there. Someone with experience will know when to use a sail and when to use rowing in order to sail the boat. Not only that, the same person will let you know about side streams which runs short to reach the end point to get in the bus without getting wet. Thus, it is very important to have someone behind you watching and observing your activities to let you know which tern to take next as well as how to achieve a given task without much effort while making it is sort of fun to work rather than sitting. However, if you got a guy in your back with nothing and he thinks that you are a threat to his well-being ....oh boy you are going to enjoy a one hell of a ride or an experience which will make you an insomniac.

Okay now to the story again; what I was telling you? Oh can we go back there? Yes I want to tell you about the tea cup and read it first. It is a story without an author, but worth reading and the moral of the story is as it says you need to go through so much of pains, so much of hardships before you become a skilled employee with competency. Okay back-again another ridiculous question; what do you mean by competency? It is as management explains; the knowledge of a something you can gather within few, which will apply for a certain time for training and then another time slot for making or caving it to a skill in you. With the experience you collect while applying it, you will become perfect or near perfect user of the given skill where you become a competent person. Thus, you know that you can't achieve it without following someone's guidelines so easily, where you need to learn the next secret of surviving in corporate world which is "you need to follow in order to lead someday" that is a well proved old adage too.

Now let's get back to the story of "TRIALS OF A TEA CUP".

I haven't always been a tea cup. There was a time in my life when I was just a lump of clay. Then one day, my master took me and began to pat, mold and shape me. It was very painful. So I begged him to stop, but he only smile and say "Not Yet".

Then he placed me on a potter's wheel and I went round and round. I got so sick, I thought I wasn't going to make it, but then he finally let me off.

Just as I thought I was going to be alright, but my master put me in an oven.

I have never understood why he wanted to burn me. I yelled and begged for him to stop, to let me out. I could see dimly through the glass on the oven door, but he only smiled, shook his head and said, "Not Yet!"

Finally he came and took me out "oh! That sure feel better" I said to myself.

Then all of the sudden, my master picked me up, where he started sanding and brushing me. Then he took a paintbrush and started painting colors all over me. The fumes were so strong where I thought I was going to pass out. I pleaded with him to stop, but he continued to smile and said "Not Yet!"

Then he placed me in another oven, this one was twice hot as the first.

I knew that I would suffocate. I begged, I pleaded, I cried, but he still only smiled and said "Not Yet!"

I began to feel there was no hope, I would never make it. I couldn't take any more. It was all over for me. I decided to give it all up. Then all the sudden, the door swung open and master said "Now!"

He lifted me up and he placed me on a shelf to rest. Later he came to me with the mirror and told me to look. As I looked at myself I couldn't believe my eyes. I said, "Oh my! What a beautiful tea cup"

Then the master explained "I want you to understand that I knew it hurts, when I fatted and molded. I knew the spinning wheel made you sick. But if I had left you alone, you would have dried up there and always have been just a lump of clay.

You would not have had any personality in your life." "I knew it was hot when I put you in a first oven, but if I hadn't, you would just have crumbled".

"I knew it really bothered you to be brushed and painted, but if I hadn't, you would not have had any color in your life".

"Oh, how I knew the second oven was so hard for you! But you see, if I hadn't put you there, you would not have been able to stand the pressures of life. Your strength would not have lasted, so would not have survived for very long".

"So you see, when you thought it was all so very hard, I still had you in my care. And you all along what you would be today. I had the finish product in mind from the day I first touched you!"

Author unknown

All of us have to go through pains in life; if only we understand that each such pain is making a better person out of us, our day will be better.

Okay, now you know what master and the tea cup as well as how he moulded the ugly sticky clay ball in to a nice tea cup. In the same way you will find someone in somewhere like to mould you into something, my advice is, just take it and try to act calm even if the guy is so embarrassing to you. Just observe what he is trying to pull you up to and if there is something promising or if you can predict something in immediate future just grab it without waiting while being pessimistic.

Now let's sum up with what we came across and see it in another perspective of training where you will make hundreds of mistakes before you start doing things accurately. However the problem is, if you start without having a mentor or self-guiding to follow what others done in the past, it will be an embarrassing experience and you will run-out of your career even before you start it. Hence, it is always better to find someone you can trust with experience, willingness to share and passion to mould others.

Obey the Rules

You are not in Kansas anymore, you are on Pandora,
Ladies and gentlemen, respect that fact, every second of everyday.
If there is a hell,
You might want to go for some R & R after atora on Pandora.
Out there beyond that fence,
Every living thing that crawls, flies or squats in the mud want to kill you and eat your eyes for jujubes.
We have an indigenous population of humanoids called the Na'vi,
They are fond of arrows,

Dipped in neurotoxin that will stop your heart in one minute,
And they have bones reinforced with natural occurring carbon fiber,
They are very hard to kill,
We operate -- we live -- at a constant threat condition yellow.
As head of security, it is my job to keep you alive,
I will not succeed, not with all of you,
If you wish to survive, you need to cope better strong mental attitude; you need to follow procedures...
You got to obey the rules, Pandora rules,
Rule number one,
"It is like an old school safety briefing to put your mind at ease "isn't it?
Okay guys do you remember this safety briefing somewhere? I'm pretty sure you did, it's the first thing Jake Sally listens when he arrived at Pandora; this was one of vary famous films back in 2009, that was done by James Cameron, Canadian born famous Hollywood film maker. "The Avatar"; why did I took this pieces of little dialog, because this is what you need most importantly in your job, discipline and you got to obey the rules.

The rules came into the world because of the wars, which you hate, but fortunately most of the sophisticated technologies lay their eggs due to the human war mentalities, where soldering became one of the very first jobs like prostitution. Now think about for a moment that if you do not consider to obey rule of the battle field what will happen to you, indeed you know that you will die, but in the industry?. . ? . . ? Yah you will not die, unfortunately you will not succeed either. Because the moment you join the company, you are bound to look from company perspectives or in very simple words you need to look out from your boss's eyes or company owner's eyes. The moment you failed to do so, you will get noticed and that will be a black mark for your carrier there, because as I always say; you will be paid for your hard and good work at the end of the month and it will be forgotten. Nonetheless, all the mistakes you did and all the failures you had within the month will be continued to the next month. In other words, we only carry forward our mistake into the next month in any company, but you never carry forward much weight of whatever you did well in the last month. This is a well-known fact and everyone neglect it.

> **Behave, be disciplined and be positive.**

The survival is very hard today in job environments, because it is very challenging and people come to job in order to get paid but not to work, this is one of the major disorders in current techno-prick society. It is better to keep in your mind that, you are there to serve your employer and he is the one who pays for your dinner and no one else. How harder or smarter you work or even you don't work is not very much important in a company, but obeying the rules and pleasing your bosses are very much important. Literally you sold 40 to 48 hours of your day time per week to your boss at the moment you signup the job contract with the employer, where it is your first duty to satisfy him or her about your behaviour. How you work, how you walk, how you talk, how you drink, how you treat and the way you approach people within an organization is very important, because, these things are always noted by your superiors in the hierarchy. In fact, when I have a trainee or a new subordinate we always look how he walk, talk and behave in the society. The general acceptance is that, if you are walking fast most probably you are working fast too. However, there are fast walking lazy fellows in the society too, where you always can't expect the same typical model all the time.

> **If you obey all the rules; you will miss all the fun -Katharine Hepburn.**

Okay let's talk about another story, you remember our pal, Mr. John, who was a very hardworking character and a best performer in the company, where he had very few friends and lots of enemies due to his fast faceted multichannel development process for face lifting of the company. As we earlier discussed he had almost completed the system and half of it was implemented and planning to finish it within few months to come. Even though he is highly skilled, experienced and high tech character, he was also an acentric straight forward man who cares no body. He was following his CEO's orders and CEO loves him very much, but it was another reason for others to hate him, because he parses him in front of everyone while shouting at the others. So he was really motivated because of his boss's behaviour and he worked further hard. However, there were forces which were much stronger than he thought.

One day there was an audit for the factory, an auditor came in and while on the way auditor has call the John's boss II, the son of his CEO. He was very lazy bully character, who said that he has learned lots of marketing and business administration in a developed country, then back as a director without any kind of exposure to the environment. His management model runs through asperse or backbite where he has some favored people whom he uses to skim the company people and to find out what they are talking about him. Unfortunately, he was amalgamated with the most unskilled people who always tend to wash other's dirty linen in-front of the director to get the credit, and they were somehow efficient with their production figure by utilizing almost all resources that can be used, where director thinks they are much better than other workers.

So this guy was not a fan of john because he didn't like his nonsense stories and achievements since everyone knows he has done nothing rather than siting and talking there. He doesn't listen to anyone, yet others have to listen where he was managing one-way communication without letting others to talk. Now this auditor called him on the way and he found it when he wakes from the sleep at around 11.30am which was his usual time of waking up from the bed. He immediately call the john and asked him to not to show anything of the factory fearing that auditor will himself start this business or will tell someone else how to do his father's business.

Thus, john was in a difficult situation and the auditor was from a third party certification body and he was assigned by a supermarket chain to evaluate the quality of the product as an annual event. The auditor was in-front when the call came and now as he was instructed he can't tell anything to auditor, yet auditor demands his right to know policy because that's what his job was, where supermarket chain is completely depend on his recommendation. However, John didn't want to make him upset either so he shows the plant and explain the process to auditor to safeguard the order.

> ## Work Hard, Work Smart
> ## But Don't Overwork.

Now audit was over and he successfully covered with the cleverness, where there are lots of issues in the production line which was not exposed to the auditor. Yet this idiot director thinks about not listening to him all the time and later he asked John to come to his office, where he shouted him with as much of arrogance, rudeness he can find. Unfortunate poor guy, he never did anything wrong, yet he saved the order for the company. Therefore, he decided to not to talk to him again and to move as soon as possible where he was moaning for few days and remembered the theory of Boss is Boss, He is Always Right, He is an Idiot, so Get Back to the Work , and started working again.

However, his contenders were asking him what happen, where John used them to deliver the message that Boss II was even lesser than an animal. John also was an arrogant character where he didn't answer to his (Boss II) calls either. Two weeks later, he was working and his CEO was still parsing him as usual. One day, suddenly the Boss II appeared in John's office room and tried to drag him out of the gate where he said no need of such act since you can find a substitute person and I will go. So John left the organization immediately without a living or a job as well as with the loss of pride, because he didn't look from his boss's own eyes, instead he used to look from his own eyes and from CEO's eyes or to try converting others eyes to see from his angle. This was a true story and it's more longer than this and the moral of the story is that, if John was obeying the rules of the game and if he was catering to the management requirements instead of try to develop the organization he still works there, but what he didn't follow is all the orders come from the top.

That's what happened when you mess up with the rules of the game, so it is mandatory to find out major threats in your environment and to use your tactical skills to survive than development. Because if you don't survive your ass, no body there to do so for you and if you are not survived, you will not be able to continue the planned development or most importantly you will lose your dinner. Losing the current job will destroy your mental attitude and it also reduce your market value, if you are in a such situation, you better get move yourself to somewhere else as soon as possible and till that you need to please everyone for a while. On the other hand, if you start ordering others, "you need to obey the rule" as the first rule.

Three simple rules in life
If you don't go after what you want; you'll never have it.
If you don't ask; the answer will always be no.
If you don't step forward; you'll be in the same place.

In current corporate world, you get a rare opportunity to work nine to five because we're more connected than ever before, so many of us are working longer hours with more commitment on duty and off duty which corporate executives call 24/7. With this in mind, it's important to find and hire passionate people, who genuinely care about the businesses as well as its purpose where purpose is no longer a buzzword. Thus, it's a must have in your curriculum. Nonetheless, passion and purpose will retain people focused on the job at hand, which ultimately separate the successful from the unsuccessful.

How you explain the luck? Okay! try to explain it now; I know you will come up with various kinds of possible answers, because I have asked this question many thousand times from many different kind of people. Most answers are analogous to each other "Luck is Luck" what else it would be? If you read my CV it starts with following sentence "I'm dynamic, self-motivated innovative, hardworking individual of proven track records in Science and Management with special emphasis on Food Technology, Business Management & Research. I don't believe in luck, but team spirit and........" Thus, lots of interviewers asked me why you don't believe in luck, so I explain them in very simple words that "Luck is where opportunity meets the preparation" nothing else. Hence, No sane person feels ready to accept a great new responsibility, because it is only by shouldering a burden or a great responsibility that you learn to trust yourself *where you also need the pre-preparations. It's just like riding a bike; where anybody can tell you how to ride it, but to actually ride it, you must overcome your fear of falling and you need to get on to it. By the way, you almost certainly will fall along the way and when this happens, you need to try again. All the time, you start to realize what you can do next; only when you get started, because facing challenges is a valuable opportunity to get improved yourself. On the other hand, pretending is easy, but achieving is may be not as easy as you imagined, therefore it should be in a self-motivated way.*

> *Be open-minded, Be a good example to others*

According to Marshall Goldsmith in his leadership development model of **Leadership Is a Contact Sport**: *"being successful as a leader can be hard, whereas demands on leaders is increased, there is less time to focus on making the changes you need to make to do the job successfully; which is a significant challenge to overcome because as more is expected of you. Thus, you will find you have* less time for development, and yet, improving your leadership skills is more important than ever, where you have to learn on the job. In addition, it is wise idea to make the most of your surroundings, and ask those around you for help. You have to enlist their support as you do your best to develop yourself, your people, and your teams".

The Leadership Is a Contact Sport model has eight steps: Ask, Listen, Think, Thank, Respond, Involve, Change, Follow Up. Following is a short description of each step. You can practice it yourself, it gives you an opportunity to start doing something.

How does it work?
Following is an excerpt of his model:

Ask: Ask people "How can I be a better ___ (manager, partner, team member, etc.)?

Listen: Listen to their answers.

Think: Think about their input. What does it mean?

Thank: Thank people for sharing this valuable feedback with you.

Respond: *Respond positively when receiving input.*

Involve: *Involve the people to support your change efforts.*

Change: *Change isn't an academic exercise. Act on what you learn.*

Follow-up: *Follow up regularly and stakeholders will notice the positive actions you're taking based their input.*

Stay Positive or Negative?

When you start working somewhere you will very quickly realize that the work environment is a very important factor for your success or failure in the position which is always influenced by the other people's behaviours. Anyway guys do you think that this book is about positive thinking? I doubt it, because it is in most people's eyes will be negative. But it is in reality transcendence/ perfection or looking at the whole picture to *prepare yourself, rather than trying to be positive maniac, who sees the world from others eyes while trying to please them. That is what happened, if you don't consider anything about negative thinking while trying to be a positive minded person. Thus, it is very important to learn negativity and it's activity while stay positive in a tough working environment. That is why you need to learn about behavioral patterns of the work force. If you are a very good observer, you will find some of the following characters or behaviours around you:*

Bulldozers;
Complainers;
Gossipers;
Patronizers;
Whiners;
Negatives;
Snipers;
Backstabbers;
Clams;
Walking Wounded;
Controllers;
Sluffers;
Brown Nosers;
Exploders;

The next most crucial factor in a work environment is that there are two major types, the positive work environment and the negative work environment. If you have a positive work environment, you don't want to worry too much, unfortunately there are no absolute positive working environments or negative working environments, because they are reactive to each other and are in coexistence. Hence, if you expect a positive or negative work environment, there is none such work place in this world, thus you have to except both and accept both as well as need to learn how to react to both.   So if it is negative; then following explanations might help you to understand what kind of work environment is around you and what possible courses you have. On the other hand, negative world view also has a greater impact on your work environment too.

Negative Work Environment

Dog eat dog . . . everyone fighting to get ahead

No one appreciates your contributions

Too much work . . . not enough help
Deadlines are unrealistic
Longer hours . . . additional work
Budget Constraints
Competition is eating us alive
Poor management /direction
Job insecurity

Negative World View
A recent Statistic:
Crime down 20% in America reporting up
600%,
Look at what you are looking at !!!
Media Frenzy

Changing Environment
It may be difficult to change the
environment at once because as we already
discussed change is the most difficult factor
in corporate world. However, if you want to
do it, and if you do it; you will understand
CHANGE . . .

> Challenges our paradigms
> Alters the way we think
> Makes life more difficult for a
> while
> Causes Stress

Is an ongoing fact of life

> **The only person who always likes change is a wet baby**

The positive thinking is teaching us to be alive and be positive on everything, do you think it is possible? May be, but most instances it is not, because if somebody hit you with or without a reason, do you happy? Do you try to please him or try to find out why he hit you or hit him back? The last two things will happen, but certainly not the first one, so if you don't feel happy then do you think you can make someone else happy? Possibly not if you are not an insane person or cunning politician, because anyone will try to use the opportunity to his advantage, then why don't you? If you think it is negative thinking nope, it is not. According to what we discuss here it is absolutely positive thinking instead of pleasing someone else. That's where politicians come from, if you hit him, he may ask you to hit again, and smile at you and pardon you, then he will ask media guys to make a huge publicity out of it, so then he will win more votes out of sympathy. So that's why they are so cunning, then why don't you become someone like that instead of waiting for longer term solutions for such silly act of someone.

Hence, don't take everything positively, take whatever you can and don't follow the popular philosophy, then why are you reading this book, go read a positive thinking book. I have read hundreds of them and tried many of them, but I feel something's missing in the equation, that's because negativity is also important as well as positivity. Consider the magnetic fields, how they are crated? It is positive and negative poles, isn't it? So with two same poles can't create a magnetic field where there must be both in harmony, but unnecessary negativity shouldn't over take you or in other words you should not let others to decide whether you are a negative person or a positive person. Be careful of both, because if someone answers you saying that I'm fine and how are you while you see his body language tells something else, then don't be deceived by his smiling, that sort of positivity by book, so find out the negative. If he is trying to show happy pose, which means certainly there is something that he is trying to hide behind his happiness. Don't trust such guys, move your ass, be observant, keep your eyes open and mouth shut. Because people are miserable creatures and easily drop down to the ground, but they will get up later so ignore it. Don't mind who is trying to distract you, do your work; then mind your own business. If you want to be sure about these absolute positive guys, just keep eye on them, they will suffer much more that anyone, but they try to please everyone, that's the truth. However, most people who is employed for a long time in organizations will usually have following as their memories or symptoms.

Past Experiences

Most of your current actions are based on your past experiences; longtime ago, there wasn't a way like today to communicate so easily where there was no chance of shearing experiences or what we called today as lessons learned. Thus, everyone has to learn lots of things by mistakes, sometime later when these mistakes were obvious, lots of solutions created and world became more sophisticated. But these same mistakes and solutions also created lots of problems later, if the experiencing person's perception is wrong. When it comes to work, following problems are obvious.

Determinism Theory

Genetic: My Grandparents did it to me. (Inherited traits)

Psychic: My Parents did it to me. (Upbringing)

Environmental: My Spouse, my Boss, the Company, the Economy, etc.. is doing this to me. (Surroundings)

So, how do we get away from such circumstances is the most important thing. Hence, answer is not simple, but simply what you can do is Beware of the Bullets! Otherwise, even before you think, you were hit by a bullet. This is all about your attitude, and choosing the right attitude. As a matter of fact, it does not need to be exactly positive thinking person as we already discussed that there are two sides in each coin. However, change of attitudes towards shielding yourself while avoiding infection is the most important part of the game. Because, once you got infected, usually it is very difficult to cure where most probable option is to change the employer.

Ouch!
Life's Little Question:
Are some people just born positive thinkers . . . or is it their CHOICE?

So change the attitude towards self-shielding instead of getting hurt.

There is no point getting involved in others problems, or listening to others pain issues if there is no any gain for you, because this is corporate world.

It is basically like dodge the bullets or being bullet proof, because if you are going to make others problems into yours, then you are going to shake your stability, hence shielding yourself or being bullet proof will help you mind your own business. i.e., this doesn't mean that you should not listen when someone needs to tell his/her heartbreaking problem cause by others in the same working environment, but reacting against it without any incentive is the biggest problem. May be you can listen to him and try tell him how to tolerate it or some advice, but don't try to possess it or don't let them possess you, because if you do so the next victim is you, so try to wear a bullet proof armor against others attitudes.

What is so called bulletproof armor; change your attitude against the situation where your utmost important activity must be survival, hence you need to further concentrate on survival strategies while being stay transcend.

Self-change

$\mathcal{T}$he self-change is a way of neuro-linguistic programing where, it's adaptations of changes are part of cognitive and behavioural psychology. Thus, your survival or self-defense, preventive strategies and improvement (you can call it a bulletproof amour) comes from self-change.

If you really want to self-change here is little something you could follow, pick up an activity that may be anything like stop smoking, reducing your weight by 10 pounds or anything else practically challenging your comports. Then plan how you achieve desired objective and what are the possibilities and traits of following it. Try it for a while, then assess the results with a comparison to the planned objectives. Let's see if you have achieved it, but if you are trying something like this for the first time, may be you already failed or still have long way to go. Very few may have kept your objectives alive, so it is not that easy and there is a great tendency that you will fail, but if you fail still you will understand why you failed which is your captivity in negativity, so what are these captivity of negativity to achieve your future self? Okay here are some of them according to Dr. Kathryn J Lively (2013).

Lack of commitment is often the case when you picked something because someone else was doing it or they did it to make someone else happy. It practically goes without saying, but changing for someone else requirement without fully adopting it for yourself is pretty much a waste of time. This is where I already said that positive think is not exactly the path, because negativity in your mind will still have a big role in deciding what you are and who you are as well as what are you doing?

Role-strain is another circumstance which is as to the social psychological theory, a role is a set of rights and obligations that are tied to a given social position. This may occur if the demands within one social position become too much. Hence, you often failed instead of achieving the set goal, because you had so many other demands associated with being a new employee.

Role-conflict is often happens due to over commitment within one social position where the rights and obligations of one position interfere with the rights and obligations of another position. So you may tend to lose some of the commitments due to pressure from other commitments which is often manifests itself in terms of exhaustion, irritability and, eventually, burn out.

Identity issues are another trait, because you, as an individual, have a pretty good idea who you are and also, what kind of person you are, what you like to do, and how good you are at the things that you do. Often, when you fail to match your expectations of the kind of person you are or even if you surpass them, you still experience "deflection" which is often experienced as unease or as some form of emotion. In order to reduce these feelings caused by deflection, you often come up with something whatever you can do consciously or subconsciously to bring your circumstances back in line with your expectations or identity.

Failed expectations are another big issue when you try to practice positive thinking or anything that is not what you are. Because lots of people make changes in their lifestyle or working daily basis, but it doesn't always end up as they expected it would be; hence that will create lots of imbalance in your life. I.e. I have a big mouth, so everybody say you are too loud where I have tried many time to reduce my voice, but unfortunately my entire process of thoughts, way of talking, and quick reply to anything affects very badly and I'm losing my grounds when I try to do so. Thus, not any more pleasing of others while affecting my own circumstances, and now if someone feels I'm speaking too loud, I'm sorry or I ignore it or I leave their conversation. If I was thinking positively, while trying to influence others as most of positive thinkers argue; I would have hurt myself while pleasing them. So no more pleasing whether it is positive or negative. Hence, you shouldn't care either.

Because our systems are based on our capacity of pleasure, pain principle; as a consequence, if your mental pleasure is affected, then and there negativity will reject whatever it is. Thus, don't go with the popular advice, think yourself how much you can tolerate other person's bullshit, before you garb it, where it is important to be very clear on what your desired outcomes are and how they match your strategies as well as to make your outcomes reasonable. In addition, you should be willing to alter your expectations whenever necessary in the case your goal are met where you won't backslide.

Lack of social support is another major issue because of your reference group matters very much on your success or failure, where it is very important to have a right reference group, if you happen to be comparing with a wrong reference group then you will not be achieving what you want or planned. That's where you need to be a blind deaf in the case of other people's negativity issues. You listen to them, but never try to embrace them or as I already told you guys; don't try to possess. Because your ideas on what is possible or desirable, and what is worth as well as whatever sacrifices your reference group does may entail are shaped consciously and subconsciously by those closest to you. Further, it is important to choose people who will share your thoughts within your working environment instead of random friends.

This doesn't mean that you are going to be unfriendly with others or will have limited relationships, but opening up yourself as well as discussing your issues and free open talk should be limited to your relevant reference group. Nonetheless, you may have different reference groups for different environments. Conversely select good mentors, excellent achievers, or anybody that you like, but be careful to have people according to the environment. Self-change is not so easy because there are psychological mechanisms in place such as identity, privilege consistency over change, pleasure over pain and also social mechanisms such as obligations and relationships with others where it is very important to deal with psychological as well as social mechanisms in order to change yourself.

Triggering self-change will changes three things at once which are attitude, thinking and behaviour.

How to Change Your Attitude
Changes happen personally from the INSIDE OUT!

Step #1
So . . . Accept Responsibility
I am responsible . . . . . . for who I am . . . for what I have . . . for what I do

Step #2
Take Control

Ownership, values, mission, discipline from the inside.......out

How to Change Your Thinking
   Changes come from observing logically in every situation

   Step #1
   Observe Your Thinking
      What can I do to defuse this?
      This is all very interesting
      I'd like to beat the............

      I refuse to let this hook me!
      Tomorrow it will look very different.
      It sucks to be him.

   Step #2
   Manage Your Self-Talk
      This is going to be a wonderful day!

      This is going to be a crappy day!

> *"If you think you **Can**, or you think you Can't.......... YOU'RE RIGHT!"*
> *Henry Ford*

How to Change Your Behavior

Changes take true assessment, determination and discipline where you have to be passionate about what you do.

Step #1
Choose Your Behavior
Reactive - Stimulus - Response
Responsible - Stimulus - my choice - my response

Step #2
Steps toward Changing Behavior
Unconscious Incompetence....Unskilled
Conscience Incompetence.....Semiskilled
Conscience Competence...............skilled
Unconscious Competence..........Expert

The new you!

> *Lay a firm foundation with the bricks others throw at you*

Considering yourself to develop unconscious competence state in everything or situations, you are working on or at least keep trying to be, will make you a near perfect person to ask anything by anyone which will create more added value in your future career.

Influence Your Environment

Add **Positive** Behavior Replace the **Bad Habits**!

Spread a **Smile** around

Sprinkle some "**Positive**" on the negatives

Focus on the good of each day

Stay out of the "**Feeding Frenzies**"

Say "**Please**" and "**Thank You**"

Practice **Empathy**

Evaluate **Your** Behavior

Never miss an opportunity to complement

More Positive Contributions

Before you say anything to anyone, ask yourself three things

1. Is it true?
2. Is it harmful?
3. Is it necessary?

Keep promises

Have a forgiving view of people

Keep an open mind with changes

Count to 1000 if necessary

See criticism as opportunity to improve

Cultivate your sense of humor

Remember to . . .

Watch your definitions - they become
thoughts

Watch your thoughts - they become
words

Watch your words - they become
actions

Watch your actions - they become your
destiny

The choice is yours

With a Bad attitude you can never
have a good day

With a good attitude you can never
have a bad day

Choose POSI✝IVE Living

Over

NEGA✝IVE Minds

Self-Empowerment

Lots of people today talk about empowerment of workforce, but do you ever thought of empowering yourself, instead of others? Establishing empowerment in the workforce is very important, but if you empower yourself, then what is your employer or organization you work has to do; it is very simple, isn't it? They have to reword you one way or the other which is highly beneficial for the organization as well as to you. If you are a self-empowered person and if you lead an empowered group of employees, you are assuring that your team is happy as

well as satisfied with their working environment and culture which breeds better company performance that increases its retention.

Get in line with Culture

I believe empowerment is a very important concept you must first understand before you implement. At the same time, you need to understand that, it is human nature to seek satisfaction and fulfillment from their hard work. We also need to feel recognized and given credits for excellent work. Do not dismiss others work as "just" something routinely required by the organization, because going the extra mile in recognizing these talents will positively impact your company's performance and yours too.

Empowerment comes from a sense of ownership of what you do. Nonetheless, true empowerment comes from releasing the creative power of knowledge and motivation.

Think of your fellow employees as associates while imagining yourself as a person who helps link ideas and people to each other or with the organization.

Make room for your own creativity - use it with your assignments and small projects in hand. Try to help others with creativity and skills set you already got. Make room for other's creativity too - respect how your fellow employees who are creative would want to work on their works.

Celebrate mistakes and failures - do not pass judgment right away and encourage yourself to do better next time while use the opportunity to learn from the mistake. Apply the same principle for your subordinates and others too.

Set realistic expectations - understand company standards and guidelines for your work environment while explaining clearly it to the co-workers and subordinates will have a concrete guide as they work.

Engage – in both creative and non-creative endeavours. Allow yourself and others to have fun outside the job descriptions and try to make your job, is a fun work.

Reward - excellent creative endeavours, while self-rewarding is also necessary for self-respect and satisfaction, thus why don't you buy something for you or treating which exhilarate your mind.

A creative employee is a coach and a facilitator who provides support and guidance to the needy.

What is Your Brand?

What do you feel if someone asked above question, what comes to your mind when you heard the word brand? It is not a single question, Ya I know; but it is a very easy question to answer today, you will remember many different big brands like Microsoft, Apple, Google, Mc Donald's, KFC, Coca-Cola to name few for the second question. However, I know that it is not very easy to answer the first part of the question. Actually, what is a brand? Basically it is an image appears in someone's mind when you call some specific word, image or anything. In other words, a brand can be a name, term, design or other feature that distinguishes one seller's product from those of others in terms of modern trade where brands are used in business, marketing, and advertising.

Originally, the livestock branding was started to separate one person's heard from another's by means of a distinctive symbol burned into the animal's skin with a hot branding iron which helped lot in those days to solve lots of troubles. One of the modern classic examples of a brand image is Coca-Cola which belongs to the Coca-Cola Company. When you say Coca-Cola, even a small kid in the current society will feel a nice glass bottle or a can with white coloured name as well as a caramel coloured sweet flavoured liquid.

Maintain Your Status

On the other hand, there are other meanings to the brand; in accounting, it is considered as an intangible asset where brand owners manage their brands to create shareholder value through brand valuation. Each brand has a monetary value which is very important in marketing type investments where current marketing trends are to focus on long term stewardship of branding and valuing it. That's why lots of contract manufacturers are earning pennies while brand owners enjoy around 30% of the product value just by selling without doing any other thing in the market which you can recall as "brand equity". The brand equity is the value earned by the brand in the marketplace where high equity brands has higher value, which is not clearly understood yet but it has the ability to create some positive differences of the consumers mind and in the marketplace.

This will remind you that of a brand is an acronym, name, sign, sound, trademark, taste, logo, colour or any other brand element which will easily remind in the minds of consumers when it was recalled, heard, seen or shown. Nonetheless, brand delivers a trust or guarantee of the product which sells under a given brand about its expected results by the consumer. In that way, brands are creating trust and goodwill based market where consumers are repeatedly paying without doubt in mind.

Now, I gave you some background information as well as some good idea of a brand. Why? Because I know all of you are not much familiar with word "BranD", thus before you are going to understand about your brand and to build a new brand for you in the future, it is mandatory to understand what a brand image is. As a startup employee, you may think that you have no brand at the very first day you enter the corporate world. No, it is wrong, you are making your brand by first day and you always need to remember that "The first impression is the best impression that you are giving to anyone", because people will remember it for a very long time. It is very simple through, you don't need many tools, just be nice to everyone, but keep your eyes open while your mouth is shut.

I think you know about best dressed gentlemen as well as pretty women, you always need to be one of them and always dress appropriately according to the situation while been nice and clean with neat garments always. Then always vigilant about the stuffs you are assigned for, because it will be your responsibility to deliver assigned work before deadlines. It is always good to be before the deadline and to be vigilant about the quality of the work you completed. Let's say you are given a documentary work for the sake of the argument, now you have compiled your report and completed it. But did you read it before you submit it? Did you check for the spelling mistakes, grammar, flow of the sentences, how it was arranged as well as the template of your document? In addition, you need to check pervious reports of same kinds if it is the first time you are doing it. If you have done all this, fine.

Never say Never

Tomorrow you get another report from your boss and may be more, now you think you are branded as a documentary clerk sometimes, oh hell no! They recognized your potential on documentation and they are going to use you for such purposes when something important come across. Now in a way you are branded as a good report writer with good skills. I use this example because most of the school leavers can do this kind of stuff without any training since they are very familiar with computers and word handling software than older generations.

There are many other avenues like this, what you want is only to focus on the given work while showing that you are a reliable chap for such assignments. It will not limit to any specific field and can be applied to anything. The only thing is that, you always try to make some impressions in others mind by completing a given task within deadlines as well as perfect results. You also need to train your language, style, and passion to match the job function you are assigned. Building a personnel brand is not that easy. However, when you do that everyone will rely on you for specific expertise and people will make references on you. Even after you are gone from a company, people will remember you for the works, passion, fashion, behaviour, achievements and so on. You may be worried that, it is hell lots of works that I'm asking you to do, but it is not; where you have to do is improving your day to day works while perfecting it.

Have a plan – daily, monthly and yearly

I prefer telling stories than writing about some topics like a writer, because I know you are not going to remember it. This is the very essence of your future, where you need to follow it up. I always wanted to be an all-rounder from the very beginning, because I was targeting to be an investor someday, based on that long term plan, I hunt down many things came across and today whatever the company I work, people on top always prefer to see my opinions in any matter without limiting to food science or quality which are my comport zones. Not only the company I'm working, but many other my previous working places, my clients, and friends or colleagues ask for little helps that I never says no, that's what my brand is.

I always prefer to work in challenging positions rather than working in my comport zones, because you will learn nothing in your comport zones rather than teaching it to others. Sometimes engineers come to me asking about recommending machineries to the plant, do you think I'm joking you, Nope! That is some other person's comport zone, but I have some solid experience in application of such machineries where people tend to ask my opinion. Now, you need to remember one thing; I'm not an expert in that field where I may not know exact formula or some complex calculation to redefine a machine. On the other hand, my knowledge on application may have different dimensions where you need to tell them what you can properly tell while telling them that what you don't know.

It is a good thing that, you need to tell people about what you exactly know as well what you don't. Otherwise you will lose your reputation by telling lies and showing off what you don't have. That will not be a good image for your personality, whereas it will be a suicide. On the other hand, you should have character of been the same honorable person every day while keeping your judgments impartial. Don't go washing dirty linens of other people in front of your boss. Instead attack the same person with full power, but be logical and meaning full, always prepare for the worst. Attack in the front, instead of being a backstabber where you will become a more straight forward person where lots of people will honor and love that attitude, even though lot too hate you.

Once you create such background around you, the situation will brand you itself rather than you try to promote yourself. Then people will remember for what you are and what you do. Once your crate your own brand around you. It will value you, but most difficult part comes next to it, because once you achieve the recognition there are many people to criticize your attitude. Hence, maintaining of what you have earned will be not easy where you need to stay focused and tuned all the time. However, creating your own brand is an individual task where you need to carefully select the circumstances.

> Minimize errors; do not give others' the satisfaction of criticizing you

Do what you say; Say what you do

Okay guys, what do you know about standards, do you ever come across a standard? I hope you did, because we all need to follow some rules in life; at least if nothing, the jungle law. Okay what is the jungle law? Do you have any idea of it? I hope so. The jungle law is of survival of the fittest, which was also renounced by Charles Darwin in his famous theory of Evolution (On the Origin of Species) where he called it as "Natural Selection". Thus survival is discussed in many occasions and it is the most innovative thing in the world that changes from one thing to another without notice.

Do you know why I asked this question and still continue to talk about it, that's because this was the first rule in life; you have to survive whatever the circumstance it is. Hence, rules were first made and they were further expanded as well as improved by time which later became standards. If you consider the ISO 9001; it is one of the well-known standard for management of quality of work place and manufacturing system. Nevertheless, it initially started as a part of military purchasing guide due to low quality products supplied by defense suppliers which was later converted into a British standard and finally became a family of ISO standard. But its development and survival according to the changing industry needs as well as consumer preferences has created a dynamic environment where almost every 8 to 10 years' time, it is improved, modified and re-introduced to the market for its continuity of survival.

Thus, my question was what is a standard? Actually it is a set of rules and regulations that are established to control something, but dictionary says "something considered by an authority or by general consent as a basis of *comparison or an approved model". Either way, standard is all about setting up qualifying criteria and following according to the set guidelines.*

Okay! I have a question again, how you build your trust among the crowd? What is the most important thing in building trust among the others? I hope this will be a so easy question, isn't it? The answer is very simple; be a man of your word. Then everybody knows that you are a guy of your word, if you can do something, don't reject it, or if you can't do something don't accept it. Don't try to hide what you can't do, or accept, some people definitely may not like your so called behaviour but the most important rule you are going to build around you is to become a man of your word which will create the first rule of making a standard about you.

> *The rule number one is*
> *DO WHAT YOU SAY.*

We talk about branding you, so this is another major step of making your brand which is called standardizing you as a man of his/her word. It is very difficult, because lots of people used to lie on anything to nothing. Stopping that is not as easy as you think where lots of people don't want to do it. You personally start lying to your parents first, and then you lie to your friends, relatives, lover, coworkers, boss, neighbours, children, general public, etc. This never ends without getting caught of your fabrications and dishonored by others which embarrassed you much more than accepting the truth. Because, once you have lied to someone you may need to tell much more than 10 - 20 additional lies to cover-up your ass to keep others trusting you on what you say. Thus, why don't you take the easy step of being honest to yourself? Start telling the truth even if it is making you embarrassed and disregarded somewhat. Because, there will be a day that others starting to accept that you are an honored man who says the truth even at your difficult times.

> The rule number two is
> SAY WHAT YOU DO.

It is a very important concept which is very difficult to practice all the time, but if you can manage it, then you can go one step forward, and try the next rule of earning your honor code. When you become a truthful man then you are very close of being a man of your word. Next thing you need to do is, you have to follow your words and you have to keep promises, if you promised to do something, now it is the time to do it, because people believing in your words already.

Now you have being living according to your words where you do what you say and you say what you do. Now you are a man of your word; thus when you continue to be the same man, it become your standard, because of the trust you build around you as well as what people expect from you to do in a given situation. Now standards that we talk about before are the same, which says what it does, as well as it practice what it says and it writes what it says. Now you understand that your standard of acting to a given situation is benchmarked, where you don't need to explain others about the situation. So write down your good rules in life or in work and follow them as guidelines. But don't keep them still, try to improve and update them; otherwise they will expire soon.

> ## The rule number three is
> ### BENCH MARK IT.

Now if you apply the same principles to your working place and the job that you are doing. You are already creating a positive standard around you where people starts to believe on you. These principles are not rocket science, and they are available from prehistoric times, but nobody's applying them properly.

That's one of the reasons to create auditing mechanisms after standards are invented, thus you can do a self-audit to understand your situation in the organization. Let's say you are doing self-audit before you start building your honor code, then we can call it as a gap analysis, which gives you the understanding of your current situation. May be you can ask from one of your most trusted colleagues to explain how he sees you as whatever you are or you can listen to others, even your lover will give you a good explanation if he/she trust you. So think *about improving yourself in the corporate world as thinking it is your home for rest of the years to come.*

Hen & Turtle

Hey, are you a Hen or a Turtle? Do you understand the difference of these two people in an organization and what is the difference? I know there are lots of questions but you don't get this bullshit, do you? So if I tell you to find two of them from your current working place I'm pretty sure you don't find any of them, but I took the challenge for you after being there for few hours I may be able to find bunch of Hens and few Turtles. Why?

Because there are many Hens and few Turtles in each and every team or a company, but you don't recognize them properly till you pass sometime in an organization. The Hens are full of corporate world, and they are the people most of the time sit in top positions. But few Turtle are also there, so company will survive in any storm.

Don't Watch, Observe

I know you are curious about these two people now, I like to further increase your curiosity, which improve your observations and you may learn to be one of them according to the situation you are fallen into. But why these characters are so important, because I already told you that you need more preparations before you start a war, or if you want to survive the winter you need to make your own resources and shelter. Thus, knowing your enemy and the mentor is more important than anything else, where you need to learn about these characters in a drama or a plot. Oh wow, I'm diversifying away from the objectives; no actually I'm setting the objectives in reality.

You need to learn how to understand/read behavioural changes on your colleagues, because as I always say "there are no friends in the corporate world" and then you can be safe among Hens specially. Okay why I took this two animals as examples? If you think somewhat mindfully, you will realize actually. For a comparison if you consider these two animals, there is a big difference; the Hen is louder or noisier while Turtle is almost completely silent.

Oh! do you get it now? I'm kidding you guys; the biggest difference between them is very simple, whereas Hen lays a single egg and she shouts lot loudly to inform everybody that she laid an egg because she may needs the attraction of the Cocks. On the other hand, Turtle lay over thousand eggs and she don't even make a meek sound while disappeared into the deep sea after hiding her eggs. Now you got the main difference between these two types, where you need to mark such people who do a very little work, while showing it to everybody in the process of trying to make advantage over it. At the same time, you also need to understand who do the great work while making no noise, because these points are necessary to pinpoint your mentors and competitors as well as to share your thoughts.

But if you consider Hen and the Turtles, there is another difference, that's why they make up in the ladder better than the Turtles. Hens are laying eggs every day for a few weeks; then rest for a while before start again. Nonetheless, Turtles lay eggs only once in season and rest for a long time before a new season. So they are always go unnoticed than Hens in an organization, because her boss sees at least single egg daily and he knows it because of the sound as well as egg is laid in open. However, when it comes to Turtle, she don't lay eggs every day, make no sound and nobody knows where she hide it either. In comparison, even though it is a huge amount compared to Hen which worth much more than Hen's life time work, it still goes unnoticed where no appreciation is guaranteed.

Do you like to know my opinion! I basically like the Turtle; but I disagree both behaviours, because you need to have little show and great work both. In corporate world, you don't get the rightful ownership without a little show, because there are many on the ladder to grab your credit into theirs, in the moment they realize the importance of your work; specially your immediate supervisor, whoever you are directly responsible or reporting to.

Don't try to boast yourself which is temporary. Try to be the popular guy with more accurate great results and no boasting.

> Better late, than Never

*H*ey guys, what do you understand
from this topic? I already made some
comments on these three words, but I like to
talk little bit more about it. Do you
remember, I was telling that the way you talk
as well as the way you walk and the way you
work has everything to do with your future?
Let's consider the corporate world or the
killing space with lots of politics, sex, alcohol
and money in it; the way you have behave

within this space is entirely different, because it is going to affect your career lot from the beginning of your employment. The employer is always looking for something wrong in you, it doesn't matter how much he likes you or how efficient you are helping the company to get growing.

Be Punctual, Be Trustworthy

The instinct of the employer always works vice versa to you, because he is the only one going to lose everything in the case of business failure or a bankruptcy. You will find another job in somewhere, you may be facing lots of financial and social issues temporarily, but not permanently which will be sorted out by the time. However, your employer will not be facing the same situation because he may have to payback all the employees, loans, taxes, and many different burdens in life. Not only that, he may lose many other his properties and businesses that he holds due to one single failure. The bankruptcy may have happened due to one of the small or big mistake done by you or may be your subordinate where it is natural for your boss to closely observe you.

Thus, his instinct always filled with curiosity, without that he might have not conquered this far. Consider one of the best employees in the company and think about him. Does he holds anything much more than his salary and the perks he gets (there are exceptional cases like share issues for experts or CEOs while forming companies, who is out of our discussion since you need to go through the ladder before you earn anything as a startup)? If possible request him to go and negotiate for a salary increase from his boss. You know the immediate answer, and he will say no as well as he will not ask his boss ever because you persuade him. The moment he asked for it, whatever his good work become less okay for the boss. For the practical reasons, he don't want to keep him any more in the ring either, that's the nature in the working environment today. Because everything depend on the profitability, whatever good you have, will not be that much valuable to your boss if you are too expensive, since there is no much profitability for him. Usually, top most people get paid well, but the burdens in their heads are always much bigger than they get paid.

I like to consider myself to tell you a story, whenever I was call for an interview and if I'm not feeling right about in my instinct. Then while on the interview, if someone asked me to tell myself usually I start my answer like this, "I'm a rolling stone, but to make it short, I'm a jack of all trades and master of many, where my CV has given you all the important works I did in the past as well as what I'm. Out of given context, I will tell you what relates to the position on demand". Do you think that this is a very good start, oh..! No obviously not, that's because the moment these words come out of my mouth, interviewers understand that I'm in control and going to dominate the interview. However, if people really interested to listen, then it is become more interesting and the odds are in favour, but I hope the boss will not like me from the moment I start, because he know I'm fearless bastard, who has no discipline or loyalty.

Nevertheless, he fear I might influence his good obedient workers to become fearless like me, so I'm out from the first interview which save my time instead of wasting time with them until the last to decide. But if you want the job, you really should not make such debuts at the beginning. However, there are situations that some people will like you, because of the attitude you pose out there, since everybody cannot make such debuts and even if they did so, if you are not a real jack of all trades or jack of all trades and master of none you will fall. Thus, it is very essential to mind your words always, otherwise you will lose even before you start. Nonetheless, you got to talk to them first, as your first step toward getting employed, where you need to be well disciplined and chose your words carefully while you answer.

Have background knowledge

It is always good to research the company before you reach there. Try to find out what products they did or the services, how they are different from others as well as what sort of person they are looking for, however I'm not going to discuss about how you need to get prepared for an interview or how you need to face it. There are hell lots of information, given by many subject experts related to HR functions, recruitment interviews as well as basics of facing interviews. Hence, it is your duty to search the web or read some books related to this topic. However, my experience is that, those things have very little use when it come to the real world, because your interview is a time specific initiative that is tailor made for your appearance and their requirement. The best person in the interview mostly do not get the job, because lots of companies do not need a consultant, they just need an operator who will follow the instructions rather than creating his own.

The next important point is how you walk. If I'm in an interview panel, I usually like to have some space for people to walk in to the interview room from the door of entrance or else I will sit somewhere I can see them coming to the interview before they enter to the room. Don't you think it is important? It is very important because it tells you many things about the person you are going to interview, just look around you and concentrate on people's walking styles, don't you understand something from their walk; I hope you did. Because you are only telling us less than 40% about you in an interview, rest of the story tell by your body language, how easy you sit, how easy you face the interview questions, how easy you talks and if it is natural or not as well as whether you lie and so many other such instinct are given by your body postures than whatever you talk in front of another person.

Hence, your walking style is very important, if you walk lazily towards an interview board, you are going to lose your job even before you start the interview, because current corporate world is more efficient and fast moving, where you don't have a place in it. Further, if you are a slow walker, always remember to make it little much faster than usual and when you start your corporate carrier always mind about it. Even if you are not a very smart worker, still this small strategy will give you some survival.

As I remember some time ago, I hired a graduate with exact qualification and understanding on the subject, because the chap had some experience related to the work. However, I had some doubts about the guy, but he was in deep financial troubles as I explored his background over the interview, so I let him come. My instincts about his walking and the interview were not satisfactory, but I offered him the job thinking that I may be able to correct him due to sympathetic reasons. How unfortunate the guy and me, because he never learns to be fast and steady as well as be accurate. Some weeks later, my boss asked me to have a chat, then I went to meet him and you know what he told me? He asked why you hire that guy, I said the reasons and asked why?

Evaluate your Progress

Then his answer was that, boss came behind him, where there was a long narrow staircase. In which he can't pass the guy. Boss had walk to the stairs while observing at his walking style. He had to wait till this guy go some distance before he starts and he even had to wait in the middle till this guy goes up because the guy was so slow and lazy walker. The unfortunate end was that, guy had to leave sometime later due to his slow and less active walking style because boss starts disfavouring him from that moment and it grew up where he was terminated. Thus, it is very important for you to show some active walking style in your life which is very good for your health and also for the survival.

The next important point is the work, I kept it to the last because, employer will not see your work at the beginning but, only your exaggerated boasting CV which is not the real image of you in most cases, followed by your boasting exaggerated talks. Thus, some interviews are planned with some example work or trial i.e. driving test before recruiting someone as a driver. Since, you may be able to talk nicely and walk fast as well as show some standalone characteristics, where people may hire you. Yet you have to unleash yourself while showing your skills and need to become one of a most wanted employees in the system. To do this, you need to learn fast, walk fast and be accurate as well as smart which is the easiest survival strategy for anyone.

Once you enter to a new job, the most important thing is to learn thoroughly about the organization, its products and services as well as its people. Use your first three weeks for this; use additional hours after work, while making sure you learn quickly and accurately as soon as possible, then try to apply learnt knowledge on your work. Study how things are happening around and try to adapt in to the situation where you will find your survival quickly. We will discuss several different strategies about survival later, however, this is one of the most important thing in the corporate world. Less you tell about you to the others, much better, but you need to make sure you are getting on with everyone while creating a specific space for you within the given environment. Then only people will talk about you even after you are gone, where they will remember you for your skills, knowledge, and work or even for your cruelty over the others. Think about Hitler, or Spartacus or Caesar for different perspectives of their work. They are remembered as legends as well as history for their work whatever it is, nothing less nothing more.

> **Be quick and accurate**

God of the Arena

Have you read about Spartacus, or watched the TV series, I hope lots of people have time to look at it or read it, which is Roman history. He is more popular for doing the impossible. One of the first freedom fighters against slavery. How this was started, so go look at the TV series or read the Roman History. It is a very different story from other wars since it was based on love.

The other war based on love, we read was Trojan War which is a Greek mythology. If you have watched Spartacus, you would have come across various plots drawn from the slave maters to keep their head upright or to make their gladiators winning. Thus, you need to learn about plotting too, which is an essential skill you need to master in one way, but it is much better to learn strategy than plotting because it helps you understand the circumstances. As a very vital strategy, you can learn Game Theory which has many different ways of responding to a same dilemma as well as to use it for your benefit.

There are various strategies that you can learn according to your situation, it may be for marketing, may be for politics or even it may be for war. However, this topic is not about them, but about your learning strategies and how you can easily gain the required knowledge related to your employment or the works in hand. At the same time, learning gives you much more resilient position when you are placed in an environment, where lots of people do not read much or read but bullshit like novels, religion, facebook, other social media networks, cookery or something not very important. I don't criticize any of them, but trying to make a point; because your reading of novels or religion or cookery will not give you much of a strategy for survival, it may be to a certain extent sometimes, but not that much. So you need to learn about corporate world, if you are going to be there for rest of your life, whether you are going to be an employee or an employer, you need to have a hunger for reading and studying new things every day, which are relevant to your day today works.

> **Give your best and great will be your reward**

Okay, if you want to know something that you don't know, what will you do? I know it is an easy answer today, just go to the net, simple and easy answer is that. Actually when you go to the net who is running the show? Whether it is laptop or mobile; it is the very simple name, the GOOGLE. How they become that much successful, because they provide free information with platform for free data addition to the internet and release many open source software platforms like chrome, android, maps, earth, play, fit and so on, they have many different free platforms that people have free access with options for data uploading which other people can use it for free or you can retrieve later or process it.

Thus, if you want to learn something new or want to understand the basics of anything, just google it, that is the term people use for it. When you get in to the google, the best source of basic information for anything will come from Wikipedia, which is the most reliable source today since it provides you with many citations as much as possible where you will have the access to those links and decide yourself if it is okay to believe in it. You have your mobile connected to internet, I hope you always look at your facebook page, find time to chat with your partner, friends, family, colleagues and many other based on your circumstances. You may also use emails, other sort of many data platforms such as viber, what's app, pinterest, twitter, linkedin and so on to have some fun within the spare time you have. Thus, I suggest you to use this time for your own benefit and to your advantage, forget about bloody facebook which is a waste of time, try to go to google and try to learn something interesting. You might not interested in game theory, but you may be interested in how your company's production line operates and what sort of new equipment you can use for easy operation in your current job or how company's production system really work inside. Nonetheless, you may find several new things that you can explore when you enter the free data space, which do not have limitations or boundaries.

Maintain a "to do list"

Hence, it is your own will that lead you to the top of the mountain, no one will take you there unless otherwise you don't have a free will. However, when you start to learn from the google, it will be so easy that, because it is paper less space and you can read many things at a single opportunity. Let's say you go to Wikipedia; you may be reading on a single topic. While you read, you will find out that there are several links to many different words which are, if you click, it will lead you to some other different pages instantly. The newly open page will also give you sideline information on a different term or an activity etc.

Therefore, it is advised to read relevant sidelines, which will enhance your knowledge while expanding your memory. Youtube will further give you insights to the matter as well, this will go on and go on. When you create your own interest you will not stop it, that's where your basic skills can be polished into something that none of your teachers or mentors or boss can do. Now you know who the god of the arena is; it is google god, these days' people call it so for the joke, but I find it is not a joke, because any of your gods can't provide such help which google provides you. So try to use it wisely where you will have a good assistant all the time around you. Hence, it is very wise to ask from the net before you go to any one, which will be more convenient for you while others will not have the opportunity to spot your weakness. This is the easiest way, so grab it, which is free.

In addition, linkedin is a professional network, where you can learn hell lot of inspiration, motivation and professional online help in some of your day today issues. There are bunch of hired nice writers, they looks like daily users, who has built large networks around them and they are discussing and selling the site while in the network. Thus, if you have no such plans to be a someone like that, I don't think, you should be there for not more than few minutes a day or just to update yourself, it is much better site than facebook, but not very useful either, if you are purely targeting to find the next job. Nonetheless, it is a good place to build a smart CV of yours, where lots of head hunters are mingling around. The site has lots of options to build a smart CV, at the same time system rates your CV, it also send you the employment opportunities available.

Too much of anything is not too good

However, you should not overestimate that it is the best place to find a job, I see every day that people claim that they were doing everything in the linkedin, and following all the instructions given by the community and so on, I even have talk to some guys and try to explain them that it is just another commercial add based social network, where you should not concentrate too much of your weight on it. It sometimes give you opportunities to face interviews, but it is not the website responsible for your job, but solely you. Hence, my advice is that, use it to build a smart CV where all your certificates, research papers, any other testimonials you can connect.

On the other hand, you also can connect with people in your same working field. However always try to have people at least bit higher than yours in positions on seniority, because they will connect your CV to other professionals in the same field through their contacts, which goes on and on. It will give you an opportunity to link your CV to many different head hunters where you may find your next opportunity. Do not connect everyone, even though the system suggest for you, which I have seen many users tend to do. You may have no idea or good idea, how it is operated. These systems are backed by very powerful algorithms which suggests the relevant connections, job matches as well as daily repeated mails inviting you to the *platform. The platform want you to be an active member, while roaming through their connections and posts as your main activity. It doesn't care whether you find your dream job or not, which not very important to them. Their major objective is to increase your participations where they will find customers who will use their products or membership to increase chances of finding a new job or by posting advertisements where they earn their dime. There are various skill improvement causes, books, counselors, specialized groups and many inspirational articles there which you can depend on. In fact, if you are too much concerning on these kind of social networks to find your next ship; you will be a complete looser in most cases. Facebook, Instagram, and many more social networks also have almost similar mechanisms, which make you are an addict of their grip. Not only those, most of all networks are buzzing at us, asking us to come and play, but it is you, who should consider that if you are not using them wisely, you just lose you time and money.*

*D*o you remember a film called The Employer, of course not, even if you did; I know you don't try to remember it because it is not important and it doesn't make any sense to you, does it?

Okay why I asked this, because I wanted to tell you another story. That's about interviews and their requirements sometimes employers look forward to listen from you and at the same time to stress the job market in the future. Do you know that almost ten billion people will be coming to the dinner by the summer of the 2050 and it will not be an easy task to feed them in that dinner where it will be more difficult to find a job than today. Because there will be more people to compete for the same job opportunity, and different candidates will fix different prices for themselves, where it will be more difficult to sustain in a job, thus the price paid will be much lower than today.

But do you think it will happen, yaa! I bet and you don't; because the price of everything will sky rocketed where salary will match the living as it happens over many centuries. But if the tax rates are increased in the same way and if there are many candidates in an interview with high price fluctuations mark on their heads; it will not be a possibility. Because current price fixing is almost on individual basis where your boss may receive half of the salary you receive due to the technical expertise you hold and the reputation you developed in the industry coupled with your education. However, if you consider the single factor such as education which is almost equal for any person having the same qualification, then the selection will be flat. But in reality it never happens because the intelligence, aptitude and the attitudes are totally different to one another. Someone may grab something by looking at it while some other person will take a month to do the same.

> **Be smart, Once in a while; dodge the ball and let it pass.**

Thus, it is very important to understand about your role in an organization; whether you are a janitor or a director; it is not that important. The most important thing in a job role is quickly adapting to the environment and surviving yourself without falling into the traps laid there. What we call it "The Game of Survival" is the most important thing while making sense the company, that you are one of the most wanted persons in the clique.

Now let's get back to the story for a while; there are five candidates selected for a position in a company call kcuchario corporation and their characters are way different from one another. The day they supposed to be in the final interview, they all had been kidnapped and were locked in a *single room where there are five door locks in the single door. In reality, they have been offered 5 outgoing calls with a phone. Police can't trace them, where there is no anything to support them to get the hell out of that room without killing each other, but their instincts are not exactly set for it either. However, one guy has to go out of the room and the guy going out of room was the most adaptable person as well as the leader of the group and also least violent person out of the group. Thus, how he came out of the cell was not a mystery for you if you watch the film, where your suggestion will be very different too, because you definitely will say he is the most dumb person in the group and others are more promising candidates but if you really observe the film instead of watching you will see what I'm telling you. According to the interviewer of the company too, he is not the right one and there was a very promising girl other than anyone in the group. Hence, company wanted to hire her, where interviewer provide her with biography and facts about other four people to make sure she will get to the top.*

Look at these scripts I took from the film, because there is an important message for you. In future, you may have to face many interviews, get through them even if you are a just startup, you may promised you that you will stay at the company for ever, it is not the case, because even the company owner may have no intention to keep you under his control unless otherwise it is highly profitable. In the course of long run, it is better to get ready for any moment from now on. Thus, see through these questions and answers how they chose their questions as well as how candidates are supposed to answer for such time. The given scripts were taken from the most favorite candidate in the interview.

If hired you, is there anything that you wouldn't be willing to do for the company?
No, I would do whatever it takes for the advancement of this company and no question to ask.

In your opinion, what is the most aggravating thing in this corporate world for you?
I would have to say Concept of Fairness.

Because bleeding hearts that thinks everyone should be equal in the corporate world.
It just hasn't work that way and people think it should; are naïve and completely incompetent.

Now let's say there is an ecological disaster for the group of companies you handle.
An offshore oil rig is failed spilling millions of gallons of crude in to the ocean.
Consequently, there are three group own companies are potentially liable; the builder of the rig, the one that operated and company that owns oil.
You think about it carefully; how would you go about to handle it?

The answer was "*I will bury the weakest*", now I know you will ask is she crazy? Thus, it would not be you answer yet, so it will not be either way possible, where you will ask back; "sorry what would you mean?"

Thus, she will tell you how she will do it. "*I would shift all the blame to the least profitable of the three.*
Have them assure all the responsibilities and release weak shady story to the press creating

a scandal that would cost their stocks to plumage and make publicate them.

Because that will keeps attention away from others allowing them to survive.

This either could be advantage; expenses can be shifted around, group will accumulate losses where tax payment will be cuts off, bringing bigger profits for other companies.

It's just like gardening; you just weed out the weak, so the stronger can prosper".

Okay now let's get back to the topic; in corporate world everyone close to you and around you will act like friends, but always keep remembering that there are no friends in business, because nothing is personnel.

I wanted to point out these facts because current industry is looking for people who will engage their whole life and time to build some one's company. This is the turf you have to play and there is no any other way; so it is you who should play a smart game which is of cause the game of survival. Now let's get back to the point again, investors are not worried about the human resource or human capital or the naked term labour force, because their ultimate goal is to increase their capital reserves as fast as possible and as soon as possible. For that reason, they will hire anyone with proper skills, discipline, knowledge, training, experience and many other things which we call altogether competency.

The competency will not come to you with nothing, it is very hard labour as well as sweat of the people and it is the most important thing in the industry where you need a good reputation to be a driving force of an organization. But at the same time, you also need the adaptability to the environment which is utmost important, because if you can't survive there, there will be no job for you. Then we don't need to talk about it and you need to find another job before we discuss your survival and adaptability to the environment. Thus, it is better to hold the grounds, until you find a sanctuary to play your game and it won't be so soon that you will find it either the case, because you need more competencies than you think to reach there. So let's look at one of the last pieces of the conversations I pick for you from the same film which will explain you short and sweet what is the corporate world I'm trying to make sense to you.

Okay! Back again to the story; these extracts are from the guy who came out of the door finally.

Wait for right time to make the move

You are very good at adapting to new environment is that correct?
Ya' I'm very adaptable.
So if you wanna fill a job opening, create one.
Shoot him.
Is there another way??
There is not another way!!
Don't you get it?
This is the very essence of our profession; you are being given an incredible opportunity here.
For someone to succeed in corporate world, someone else has to wait, it was the game; right, sacrifice, for every cock floating in the water; there is a shark ready to eat it up.
You may have no idea what happens behind the scene, you pull the trigger and I will teach you;

I will show you free market for what it really is? An ocean of creditors, all they are looking for the next piece of meat.

All you need is to decide whether you are a shark or just another meal.

I think there are times we got our hands dirty.

So can you imagine or build the moral of the story? So watch the film first, then please try to do that, where you will learn something. That is your homework rather than just reading the book to grab some new knowledge which don't come without any practical applications.

Now as I mentioned earlier too, it is very important to be a person with very low rate of mistakes and you need to be working in teams. But when there is an opportunity to get noticed among the crowd for some good reasons showing of some of your talents; do not let the opportunity goes to another one, just take it. Let's say for argument's sake that you are a good dancer, and there is a party going on the company and someone invited you for dancing. What would you do? Do you accept it or not, I suggest you to take it. It may be the ugliest decision you have ever made, but if you go there and make a difference by adding some rhythm to the event; your performance will be remembered for years to come and people will invite you to dance which will make you a kind of popular guy in the social engagements. However, you should remember that it is a party and so many people looking at you, where you should not do any mistakes because whatever the mistake you are going to make will become your life time mistakes in the corporate world. It is better in such an event to go to the dancing floor; find a place where people least occupied and then start your characteristic and specific dance. This is very small example of the part of game, thus you always remember to grab opportunities that accidentally come to you or you may intentionally create the environment which will make sure your skills and competency is noticed.

If you can make good reports about anything why don't you send some small reports about some way of cutting down the cost or even improving an existing product? When you send some important reports to the management; you always remember to address it directly to your boss who ever your immediate supervisor is, but always never forget to copy it also to his boss if there is nothing against your supervisor and always try to do it through email. That way you keep a record telling that it was your original idea and anyone in the company will not credited for your finding. On the other hand, if you do not make it copy to supervisor's boss, then it may be probably become your supervisor's idea and he will get credited for it and he even supervise your new work which has no real credit for him. You should not be an expendable person, you need to be someone, others can rely on and even if others attack you, your competencies must over-shade those problems you encounter.

> ## If you don't have a good company, better be alone & silent

If you are a successful person, then there will be lots of people behind you to drag you from the feet as well as some others to push you down which are very natural arrogances today. Thus, as I always tell my folks that "you trust everyone, but you never trust the devil inside them" which will help you to survive and make things very less painful. If your instincts are not very strong; physiologically you are not going to survive a job for very long, considering that it is your first job and your past life was without problems. If you are a seasoned guy with so much background problems from the childhood, then you have no any chance to lose the job that you got and you will do anything to keep it that way. But if your farther is a rich man and you start the job to get some experience means that you look for something specially there and the moment you feel that you don't have it, you will leave it. So it is very difficult to retain in a job if you don't have a moral objective to keep it that way.

So if you want to keep the game up, you need to be an all-rounder and try to be an expert of the subject whatever you are handling. Try to learn all the side streams that are possible within your limits. Just don't sell your hours of a day to some entrepreneur who just pays your meal allowance. Make it a good opportunity to showcase your talents and the knowledge. At the same time, do not disappoint even if you are paid low, it is okay. You always think about the experience you are getting there. Do you know, what are the most important factors while accepting a new job? Of course you do; I think. It is the experience, position and salary. If you are grabbing some good experience and if your position is a good one, then probably you will achieve the money in the next job by selling what you earn today because your promotion and salary increment always waiting out there, you don't doubt about that, because that is the corporate world.

Experience, Position & Salary.

They will hire you by promising maximum benefits which will not be taken care of in most cases and I know you get embarrassed. But that's the industry that we are working today, it is the focus that you need always, because in the early stages of the jobs, people should not much worry about money, they should be worry about how to become a professional and to build himself as a competent person who can be stand alone in any given situation, none like others around him. That will give you more credibility and more opportunities, where your old employer, a friend or someone who has seen your abilities may recommend you to a very good position somewhere even before you noticed it. So my advice is to be patient and keep a low profile while showing your colours whenever, wherever possible. The theories behind these motives are influenced by jungle law of *"Survival of the Fittest"*.

> Grab the experience first; the money will follow you later.

Don't Hit the Enemy, Hammer Them

Now we have come across many different topics, in all of them I asked you to obey or some kind of a Neel down, I know as an energetic young guy you start hating me from the beginning. I knew that, but if you don't learn to follow, you never lead. Hence, "In Order to Lead Someday You Have to Follow Right Now". On the other hand, you need to learn the very first basics of survival before you become a killer. If you don't trained to hold a sward how can you start *fighting, because you are lost in the battle even before you start it. Thus, it is mandatory to practice survival theories first, and try to be nice to everyone. At the same time you need to learn the ground basics and how to fight as well as about your enemies. There is a famous adage "keep your friends close and enemies closer", where you need to improve your observations on environment and collect facts/information while you moving forward. Don't be a dirty linen washer, but keep collecting reliable information/facts without disclosing that information to anyone. It will be very important sometimes.*

Keep your friends close: enemies closer

In the cause of time, you will find one by one, small enemies immerge first, therefore always remember that big enemies never emerge at the very first. Small guys start against you first, then influencers, their supporters will come out of the den, it is just like a war, knights will come riding soon, but not very soon. So you need to be very careful if you are a just startup, you never know how to attack or when to attack and where to attack, because you are inexperienced right now. As a consequence, it is actually very difficult for you to identify enemy and the friend, if there is an ongoing cold blooded war, because everyone act like friends till they get the opportunity to back stab you even before you think to get the opportunity. That is one of the reasons that I tell you to be a silent storm and try to be a smart worker rather than a hard worker. On the other hand, lots of employees in the corporate world today don't understand the importance of history. So my advice is to learn history, I know you.... what a bullshit I'm talking about........, but if you know the history of a person or a thing you need to hammer someday because he hit you before, it is very important to know their history in the company, or even his pervious employment and many other things he did in the past. I think now you get to the point, if you don't know about your enemies, it is better to fallback instead of fighting.

When there are situations like someone trying to cut your throat because he wants to get the millage to achieve some position, incentive, bonus or even something very silly.

First let him does it, identify his weaknesses, don't be ridiculous, be nice and calm, learn about his movements. Try to find out his goals and objectives while waiting. Do you know a martial art called Thai Chi; it is one of the greatest arts of the ancient China, which was taught even after you achieve a black belt in your initial martial art class, like Karate, Kung-Fu etc., because it can be fatal and if you don't have the confidence of controlling yourself, you will use this fatal art where lots of people will hurt. But beauty of this great art is that, you don't attack your enemy, instead you watch how he attacks and make simple moves out of his attack to cover yourself while making his own attack will make fatal injuries to himself.

This is what I was talking about throughout this discussion, because if someone get into his own trap, he will learn two things; first thing is; he knew it was his own shot backfired and his confidence on himself will be dropped. On the other hand, he will start making scene that his enemy is not what he was thinking of and his preparations are not quit sufficient. Now you know it is very good to know your enemies and to study them beforehand as a preparation while waiting till you get the opportunity to let him down to his own trap or to let him backfire the shoot. These things you should learn first before you know how to hammer enemies.

Let's go to a little example, may be some of your parallel employee had gone to your boss and told something very wrong shady/nonsense story about you. Then boss questioned regarding it, but you don't have any proofs to prove your innocence. However, you may have other evidences that he has make some other mistake which lost few very good customers, if you disclose that information now at the same complaint handling table, he may find other avenue to cover it up or even he will turn it on you sometimes, if he is cleaver. Thus, let it go and wait till opportunity come to you, sometimes boss may start talking about the specific operation or something related to it, now it may be an opportunity for you to throw some light on the situation, thus you should not let him know exactly what you know, but you can make him curious about the situation.

My advice is that you never directly disclose the information instead let some background information which may lead your boss to find his wrong doing. So you haven't done anything but you can be happy that, without a cost you have achieved what you want. Now your boss even may trust you or start to trust you and possibly asked you what's going on, try to find what exactly you know, in such situations, if he push you, you can let him know or you can find one of his trusted key informants to disclose the information without even showing your face to anyone. I always like to tell you to be nice, but sometimes it is not enough, you need some strategic moves to safeguard yourself.

Know your enemy

There is something else too; do you remember that I asked you to be honest and do not lie. Yes you did, so you have to lie sometimes, because you just need to say what they wanted to here; not what you wanted to say! You need to be pretty good at that, if you wanted to go up in the corporate ladder. It is very simple theory that, if you agree with common norm without aggression, they tend to leave you alone without much trouble. So if you want to go unnoticed on something which has no any gains at the end of the day for your future. Just leave it, let's agree with common folks. Do not let other people know what you think of it or your opinion, if you want to go unnoticed unless otherwise there is no gain, because no gain without no pains.

Okay! do you know the difference between hitting and hammering? I bet you don't, do you? I think you have seen lots of ancient war films. Hitting is something very mild and even this can happen in between a girlfriend and boyfriend. When someone hit you, don't counterattack, let him do it if needs. Only thing you need to know is, who's mistake is it, if it is yours, then it will be better to go apologize for your mistake, if it is not like that, it would be great to forget it and wait, but always observe who is he. Don't let your information goes out without proper verifications. The difference between hitting and hammering is; when someone hit you, you are a single piece yet. Because it is a mild attack, but if you are hammered, you will be gone to pieces.

This is a different theory where professional management will never teach you; so this is common sense, if you want to give the shit to any of your enemies, it is better you brake him into pieces and find a strategy to give him a long shot which will make him remember it forever. Next time he will think twice before he attack or he may be intensify it, but this is corporate world where complainers have no long term survival. He will get marked for his problems and he will get his Thai Chi shot eventually. Corporate ladder is a very decisive place where you need to be vigilant. On the other hand, when you hammer someone, he will not be able to attack you for some time or you will get the butt shot even before you think, in such situation it is better get a break and change the employer. There is no alternative other than that if the enemy is so strong, where it is the stronghold for them and not for you.

*H*ay guys, what do you think about this topic, ... *Ah I know, usual stuff, everyone asks us to do so, did you ever tried this, I hope "yes" because we always do this, but only problem is that you don't implement it because it's always novel, where high risks are involved. Thus, you don't want to fail and tryout something or even if you want to do so, there are hell lot of barriers before you do it. Sometimes the person asked you to think out of the box may be the man, whom you can't convince or by-pass. This is a common*

scenario everywhere, but if you find the right boss definitely he might share his previous experience or may point out some of the critical drawbacks in your strategy and will let you know how to rectify it as well as the way forward with a proper guidance. This usually don't happen in every working environment, but it is also not uncommon.

Anyway, I want to ask you a question, close your eyes, then think about how you can benefit a poorer nation with most of their arable lands are under dry zone and country's 2/3 living in rural country side. The country has vast beautiful sandy beaches, changing climates within few hours of travel with very proud history and many different landscapes that are highly attractive for the tourism, inhabited by very hospitable country men. Okay prepare your answer in your mind, you can consider any method of economic activities good or bad and there are no limitations to the method. If you think that country is in a position to smuggle and prosper; you can consider it, because you are going to think out of the box which has no boundaries. When you do that, consider it to be more practical approach which can be applicable to anywhere in the world and really executable with ongoing problems, issues or changes due to globalization. I will let you know such a theory as usual in the end when I'm tired of think out of the box.

So, let's keep it for a while and think about out of the box. Frist of all, try to understand why you want to think out of the box in an employee's perspective, since our plan to find out unorthodox method of enjoying the job for a short while because there is no reason to stay in the same place for a whole your life. I think that era was gone long before, where you want to stay sharp and focus to capture the next piece of meat thrown in the market. I hope you remember that we discuss this, current trends are to jump out of the ship when you find the right time or even at the wrong time. If you are a perfectionist, you definitely need to have certain things figure out, because it does not matter how good you are, there will be a day in your corporate carrier that you were no longer an important person to the system. Because there will be a new requirement every day where new talents will be hired and someone else will be highlighted every time since your boss want to make money as much as possible than ever, and there will be new projects coming up.

In fact, you might find that there are ample new opportunities awaits outside for the same talent that your boss now does feels not very important. Forget about the company's big asshole reputation, or good will which is good old days bullshit, be jump shipper where you can improve yourself tremendously because it needs more efforts and concentration. The new working environment, new friends and new enemies with few busy months will bring you a new life for a while, and most of the boring usual stuff is gone away. Since, you need to adjust and settle down to a new working environment; you need to think out of the box to improve your life.

Be techno-economical

Once you were gone, your boss will feel sorry, but do you think he will shut down his operation? If you think so you are in dreams and he will find someone may be much less than he usually paid or someone whom he needs to pay bit more; in such points, he might remember you or even your mother if the price is so high, because he is losing. If not, he will thank you in his mind for letting him maximize his profit by even a penny. Nevertheless, jump shipping gives you courage to face situations into your advantage and there is no point being a good employee, because whatever these employers say they are still dumb assholes trying to maximize their profits while using us. This is not anymore of a personal issue, you are an item selling in the market, where you sell yourself as a skilled, unskilled or semi-skilled worker. Hence, your value defined by the workload, skills required and the availability or non-availability of the relevant labour in the given market.

Thus, if you can build some rare skills into you or if you can become an all-rounder, then you might have an advantage over the others. Then you can be there for much longer time while being an important employee. But once you become an all-rounder or a jack of all trades, you become vulnerable to any micro storm in your teacup, because everyone starts hating you, since you are intervening with other people's affairs which creates fear in other people's minds due to fear of job security or some other reason. Then you are making more enemies than ever and they are grouping against you to attack, since you become a common enemy inside the company. This is the problem once you become a jack of all trades, where you need to understand that, it is the right time for you to jump ship or start your own.

Stay within your limit

My usual recommendation for jack of all trades to start their own once they become to hold such position because you are no longer motivated by the small things you achieve or salaries you were paid. It is the time for someone to become an employer than an employee, if you don't take this point as a moment to go on your own, rest of your life will not be a very sophisticated one. If you think this is bullshit, talk to few guys, whom you think jack of all trades, they will tell you their lives not being fantastic lately in their working places. Okay guys, how about think out of the box???

Anyway, if you are not thinking out of the box and don't want to improve yourself, I'm pretty sure that you are not reading this book which teach you none as a matter of fact, we are really discussing here about the realities in our corporate world where people mesmerized with money and power. Thus, it is your own will to tryout something of your own or let it go, because current settings will only tech us to do or die nothing less, nothing more.

There are other ways of being a smart employee. Consider my own writing regards to being a carry taller which we discussed before, it is not nice to be doing it and one of the most shameful activities, since betraying others for your own gains is not fair. However, if you think out of the box, you still can study your boss and if he is really a listener to carry tellers. Be bit smart while giving him a bite; if everyone in the organization doing it, there is no point yourself practicing any standard methods. The most important thing is your survival till you find the next piece of meat to stay alive.

Hence, the strategy is very simple, **do your work very well, don't put fingers into other's businesses. Stay calm, don't make much noise; but use your opportunities to the best of your abilities and defeat others, once it is mandatory.**

Don't love the company, love yourself, because you are the most important person, not company, not the job, but salary and the perks as well as your wellbeing. I know, this is very radical thinking, but don't you think your boss think radically about money making and he has setup the pipe line to his pocket and not to yours, where there is no fairness, because you have to earn for him, his family, his any other expenses before he pays you which is very less compared to his total earnings or expenses. Okay, if your boss is not thinking radically he might not buy his personal car under the company, or he will not borrow when he realized that there is a recession is coming and the dollar going to drop sharply for next 3 to 4 consecutive years. He will get a bank loan and invest in physical assets which he will sell at 3 to 4 time higher sometime later and will profit much higher than the lender enjoying. Thus, there is no good or bad methods, so you need to find a way to make you are a finest figure with all discipline in you as a startup. Then your world is open for free gambling to try out the best deal to sell your day which is kind of a prostitution in a way, but if we don't do it, we have to starve and there won't be any dinner served tonight.

Start small and dream big

Hey dude, this is getting quit long which I don't like, because I'm not going to be tired of think out of the box, so let's get to the early question, are you ready?... having said that county is suited for the tourism because of its location in the equator and many other attractions on history, let's consider a strategy consolidated to tourism arena which can benefit rural poor. Considering the tourism industry, its main attractions are prostitution, gambling, drinking, drugs and smoking. Thus, all the standards of geographical attractions, history, foods, hospitality and nature have become secondary today as to the facts. Now do you have any idea how you can benefit poor, when the industry dominated by giant companies which are struggling to maximize their profits by having self-sufficient infrastructure for the operation. Now let me take you through crazy idea of mine which may not be very innovative or comprehensive because this is just an answer to my own question while I was put in a situation where I have to figure out a way to benefit such people in a country that people asked me every day how can we really do it.

Don't find fault, find a remedy

Let's consider hypothetically that Marijuana/Cannabis sativa/pot/weed/joint as an economic vehicle that can drive through our problem. This might not be applicable from twenty years today, because by another two decades marijuana going to be a common free ayurvedic drug available in every part of the world without boundaries, because governments will listen to the people soon. Why we consider this as an option, because people needs themselves to be sedate in some way for no reasons. Let's consider marijuana is bad drug, but when you consider, cigarettes, alcohols, cigars and other form of legally accepted sedatives or things that make mentally high or some kind of mental pleasure is a trillion-dollar industry around the world which is dominated by few multinational players with power to control this carcinogenic trade. On the other hand, there are number of other drugs and sedatives that creates hallucination effects which are more health compromising banned drugs than above mentioned. Thus, let's consider cigars, cigarettes, alcohol and marijuana, in which you think marijuana is the worst because other three is legal while marijuana is banned.

However, available scientific evidences are clearly showing that cigars, cigarettes and alcohols are much worse than marijuana on health issues. Nonetheless, it is an ancient herbal medicine for more than 2500 years. The drug was called "*Thailoda Vijayapathra*" in Ayurvedic medicine.

Okay let's consider Fiji Islands, where their traditional drink is Kawa, which is extracted from *Piper methysticum* roots, a pepper family plant that is grown in Polynesian islands which is a traditional ceremonial drink for sedation. The active ingredient is 'kavalactone' which is not good in large quantities, but if you need to feel the sedation, you need a gallon of kawa and you can flush the feeling with alcohol anytime. This is making people lazy and not a very palatable drink either, yet the country has not banned it; instead they try to sell it as an identical product of Fiji. So why don't we try the marijuana since it is a traditional herb in the country. In fact, it is one of the mildest varieties when you consider the cannabinol content in it, which is however sedating you much more than cigarettes. It will also last few hours of mental pleasure with less carcinogenic smoke. But if you smoke a cigarette, your sedative feeling was gone, the moment you stop smoking or less than 5 minutes, where you become a chain smoker. Now you got the dope with less smoke and you need another may be few hours later, but you still get only very few amounts of carcinogenic compounds than tobacco smoke since it's active compound is cannabinol non-like the nicotine in cigarettes which also includes compounds with benzine ring in it, *that creates carcinogenic compounds in the tobacco smoke. If you consider alcohols that creates more energy in your mitochondria, which has to be used as it released since you can't store it in your body; that's where you get extra energy to become a violent drunkard, that's why some people can't tolerate alcohols.*

Now considering my acentric idea, government can spot the early opportunity slowly creating throughout the globe and ban the cigarette while legalizing marijuana as a controlled smoke with several rules such as; if someone want to smoke he must be an adult over 18 years of age, hold a total medical insurance cover and then government can issue a license to buy it from approved shops in the country like in Canada, with more tariffs on it than cigarettes while using the existing infrastructures for manufacture. They also can control it through annual licensing, controlling amount of packs a person can buy per day as well as setting up authorized sellers through internet supported online portals such as block chains, which needs to be installed at every seller's point of sale to minimize single person buy more than stipulated packs.

As a tourism promotion strategy, the government can allow foreigners to buy more than local can buy based on their number of visits or similar parameter. In fact, you can attract more tourists to the country when it can become a marijuana free state, because the given country has a history and culture where they can't practice prostitution or dangerous drugs. Thus, they can't promote tourism as a niche product without something extravagant in tourist's list. Let's consider the population to be about 20 million and 30% people in the country addicted to cigarettes and 15% smoking marijuana. Then government may only attract 10% of the total, but still the tax has been doubled, licensing is established, which will definitely increase the government income. In addition, there will be large numbers of tourist arrivals for some initial years because you can buy marijuana with your passport and enjoy it anywhere none like other countries.

At the same time, the countrymen will have to have a separate license to grow 100 to 500 *plants based on their performance. With value added agriculture, they will earn handsome earnings through dry zone agriculture. Actually it can drive the nation into the prosperity, but it is not because the country grow the marijuana. It is because of spotting an early opportunity which creates a blue ocean, where you can swim on blue waters before it become bloody red and competitive. There are several points that we can create it to be a more resilient business idea. Yet I just wanted to show up, the way we think about good or bad is not absolute. There are opportunities always out there around you regardless of good or bad, yet spotting them and executing them are sometimes not possible. As to the hypothetical story, which actually can be implemented in a country near equator, but do you think it is possible, no it is not. Thus, even if you want to think bold and want to be bold. Still try to be realistic to your limitations and take decisions, spot opportunities, be real and enjoy the day whatever happens to your employment tomorrow.*

Because as I always say, you are only carry forward your balance of mistakes and wrong doings, nothing more. Whatever good, you did for last month has been paid off and settled, thus it is forgotten, unlike your mistakes. So, my simple advice is that, **be trustworthy, do your work well, be silent, don't cross others paths, be loyal to you and love yourself.**

I took this topic deliberately because most of the startups has smoked or smoking cannabis since it is a sedative of youth. It is an example of how you can think bold, not to illustrate my personal opinion on the subject.

Relax on Top

What is the purpose of doing a job and why you want a job? The simple answer is that you want money for your day today expenses, savings for future or basically for the survival. Do you want to increase the company profitability, expand the assets base or do you want to work for free in order to benefit the company? Indeed not, because we are there to earn some hard cash and we wait for the paycheck every payday. We don't even like to shift the payday for a single day. Thus, most influential factor of any employment is monetary terms where company can't buy high skilled employee of another organization for less if there is no any burning issue or fear of loss of employment. Indeed, people are really motivated with money other than anything. In contrast, all the management theories says employees can be motivated with non-monetary instruments such as gifts, word of appreciation and several bullshit, as we all know. Besides, if you don't get enough money, those bloody appreciation cannot be eaten in the night when you are hungry. So we need something sellable or money in order to survive. Hence, it is very important to consider your monetary terms and your perks when you negotiate for a job.

As we all know, surviving in the corporate world is not that easy and you will be a piece of meat for your top management. They don't care about your wellbeing, they first think about them and their category before they think about you. For their survival, they sell you at no point where you are always vulnerable to lots of threats. This is the reason we are trying to explain you various guerrilla strategies to go up the ladder to become an important person in the company. If you find your own ways of doing it, you can become a center of attention, which might be good as well as bad. Nonetheless, if you are an important person with lots of knowledge, experience and reputation in the industry, definitely you are going to be in rough seas soon. As an example, let's say you are an honest highly skilled employee with respectful character who join an NGO recently. When you are in a non-for-profit organization, which such characteristics. The NGO guys who is usually eating/burning money and lying to donors or everyone on regular basis while trying to show their big impacts. They will not keep people like you very long, oh..! boy if you are in a such job, you will no longer be there, because everyone want to throw you out since you are a liability.

Actually, they fear you, because their lies or fake results can be exposed through your work, since most of the NGO people are not really development oriented. They are really perk intended and thieves of donor money.

They may say, they have gone through DCDE audits or ISO standards like ISO 9001 or something else. But in reality, 90% of them are incapable of doing what they are doing. They are burning cash in regular basis for nonsenses and their activities are really wasteful with lots of unnecessary expenses. Thus, they don't want to keep someone with genuine intension of helping others and trying to change the world, that's because of the fake works as well as the status quos.

Initially we discussed how to become a well-disciplined employee, which is usually very important for your future, since you need to create your own image as a well-disciplined, very efficient and punctual person anyone can rely on. At the same time, you need to be isolated yourself to create your own image up and shining. In addition, you should not cross the borders without reason and need to be a soldier who obeys the rules. Do not let people know what you think of; not only that, keep your calm state, you should not get angry because it clouds your decisions, hence be a deaf if it is necessary. Rather, ignore the politics or problems unless otherwise too critical to sort out with others. Let silent control everything, be a fast moving reliable chap with intelligence. You should know whom you can mess-up and whom you can't, where you need to be silent while your works talk. Once you achieve this, people don't care much about you, because you are not a threat to them currently, they are worrying about others, so let them worry about the others, while you do your ground work. There is no time left for you to do your hard work and start climbing the ladder.

Focus, focus, focus

We named this chapter as relax, why? Do you think your heart is working continuously? No it is not and it relaxed as much as it works. Thus, our bodies are built to relax cells rather than to work, that's one of the major reasons for creation of various organs in the body specializing different functions. However, it is critical since if the specific organ dysfunctional, then entire system is gone and person dies. For such critical instances human body has created two units as preventive strategy where if one is not working; still body can rely on the other.

Likewise, there are various such example about relaxation and conditional state of relaxation. However, I want tell you a small story that I heard from one of my client few days ago. We were talking about relaxing and sustainability at the moment mix up with some project implementation. Suddenly he asked me "do you know that Hare and the Crow story", I said "no, but I heard of hare and the tortoise story" he "oh that's a child hood bedtime story and this is corporate world story". I think you may know the story, so the story was that 'there was a jungle, where there was a crow and a hare'.

So that's it, anyway the hare was running on the same path every day to find some vegetation and then running back home afterwards. Every time he run for feeding he sees the crow sitting on top of a very tall tree looking around, yet doing nothing. Hare was thinking "how that can be, I'm running every day for foods, medicine, water, from enemies and so on, but this guy sits on top of the same tree while doing nothing but looking down and enjoying all the time. So if he can do so why I can't do it", he was thinking for some time. After seen the craw for some time, one day hare decided that if he can sit and relax on the top of that tree, why I can't do that myself too. Then he went down the same tree and start to relax, where he felt sleepy and slept well like the other hare you heard from childhood story. Still the crow was looking down, suddenly a fox appeared, who caught the hare, tear apart, then ate where craw got his share after fox finishes the meal and get back to the tree top and looking down again. Okay that was the story, however, what is the morale of the story? Do you ever think about it, if somebody never asked you? I think the most important point is morale of the story because every story was told to give some hint about something which can be more understandable in a format for common folks.

The moral of the story is that, "If you want to relax, relax in a top, but not in the bottom" because you don't have time to relax when you are in the bottom, you have to climb up until you reach the top, once you reach there you are just watching what's happening around you but doing nothing, your every work has been delegated for skilled craftsmen who will do the job for you. You just look down and observing who is going to deliver me a piece of meat. Thus, if you want to relax, you need to be on the top, otherwise somebody drag you down or will let your boss know that this guy is having no works; he is relaxing or some other fairy tale about you and soon your relaxing days as well as even the job was gone by, before you even realizing it.

> **It is better to aim at perfection and miss it than to aim at imperfection and hit it.**

The next important point is that, even though you went up, top is the most uncertain place if you don't know the rules of the game as well as skills for survival. If you are fallen from the top, you have to go steep down the bottom which is a disaster where you will be down mentally, physically and financially. Thus, it is very important to find wings for you, once you reach the top. If you don't know how to find your wings it is more dangerous than you were on the bottom. Thus, you need to start finding your own wings once you reach the top. Even though you are relaxing; find that time more efficient because once you reach there you will have lots of opportunities for finding financial freedom which is the *most important aspect of freedom in globalized economy.*

The rest will follow because our intention of doing a job is to find your dinner nothing more nothing less, where your freedom begins or ends. That's why you need wings to float while falling down instead of letting it be a free fall. If you free fall, that's the end, so gliding/floating is very important to land in another safe top rather than end up like nothing. That's what crow's one of the abilities while being in the top and gliding down without energy to get the food and get back to the top once the feeding is done. You need to develop your skills of finding other opportunities which I don't want to limit for few areas where it can be another employment or a business opportunity, self-employment, etc. But whatever your resource base is, it should provide the necessary survival when it is necessary. Thus, it is very important to have wings of your own kind to support gliding once you are on the top.

Personality

Okay, as to your job survival basic lessons with the explanations and my little boring stories; hopefully you're equipped with the knowledge and the confidence to know what a job you are working on, what kind of people you are dealing with, what are the threats to your future, who are your enemies, what grounds you can hold on, and most importantly how to make your work more efficient and your skills are highlighted.

First, no person will represent all the characteristics of the objective profile of the person you are planning to make out of you. Yet what it doesn't represent will be far offset by all the things that it does represent because that will give you specific real guidance on what features you should put in, who you should follow, what your message should be. Accordingly, decide on specifics, get the best out of you, but don't worry that it's not perfect.

Second, as you progress through the process, you'll find that you've made some errors, where you are going to create and update your personality fact sheet, and then you are going to update your personality. In fact, you may change your personality entirety. All of these iterations are good, which will make things better in the long run. However, the point is that a personality building is not a one-time event, but an iterative process that involves your entire time.

Thirdly, building a personality is extremely helpful process to get to specificity, because it fosters cohesion to your environment, not just when the exercise is done, but going forward thereafter. Thus, personality is a very important part of the process. It's not just the result of the personality in the fact sheet that you designed to get, but it's catalyzing yourself to really start to think, who's this guy, and everything he does has got be aligned with the target personality. The success in a new employment is making sure a lot of planets line up at the same time and getting all those planets to line up at the same time, how do you do that? You get aligned with your objective or dream personality in the given space, and that's your personality.

Thus, I will tell you that whatever you decide to do; you need to stick with it for some time and do not give up, because things are never easy at first. But if you persist, and you really strive to bring that thought further, you become better, you become faster. You also open up yourself to serendipity and to chance that sometimes is very important. It's better to be smartest than to be the luckier in the corporate world and it's amazing where you will enjoy the journey, which is the most important thing.

When you have a multi-tasking job, which requires different skills set for each task at hand, it's important to make your personality align to all of them, but first one you are going to build is whatever you hired for, while making sure first job is well done before you do the second. Because, the second work given to you, may be an auxiliary work which you need to use for been standalone yourself, on the other hand, you should always keep in mind that without excelling at what you hired for, there is no survival for very long by excelling at the second task in hand. Thus, it is very important to complete both works at same excellence.

How do you feel about negative feedback of your work or personality? You will start getting worried about it and you might think, no I do not have this problem, but I have that problem. When should you start getting worried about negative feedback? I think you should worry about all negative feedbacks, but the very first thing is that, the negative feedback is a very good thing because you can do something about the negative feedback. Because, you can deal with bad news, but you can't deal with no news. So if something goes wrong, that's an opportunity to learn something very valuable, where you don't make that mistake again. Therefore, negative *feedback is an extraordinarily valuable opportunity and you need to listen carefully to it. Now the question is, when does it become too much? If all of your fundamental assumptions are being negated. The boss aren't going to buy your justifications or summoning under any circumstances, well that's not good. But usually, it's a matter of getting all those planets aligned as I said before, which is the survival. Whereas, it is always good to have plan B, C, D, E, F, etc. all the time where you can run away from trouble rather than being there anymore and getting discriminated. That's where jump shipping is very important and you don't need to love your company, but yourself.*

Even though we discussed about guerilling employments to get on the top, where I sometimes used aggressive words to stress you about the fact, but I never undermine the employer. Because being an entrepreneur means a lot of challenges. Thus, it's also extremely exciting, where he is making decisions every day that impact, either the development of a new product, a service, or an employment opportunity that has never existed before or new relationships between people or maybe, in the distant future, which is going to change somebody's life. To know that he actually directly responsible for it which is pretty powerful.

> ## Do it right even when no one is looking

As a startup, you will face hell lots of difficulties and hardships in your life. As I usually explain it to my trainees, you came from heaven to a piggery and became piglet before you became a craw or even an eagle. Having lived in such difficult conditions when you were growing up, you are not afraid of hardships. I think that's the kind of more important than the fact that you was suppressed, and that's where you tried to rebel. Now you are used to hardships, and you are not afraid of them, once you become an outshining personality, you actually exposes to high levels of risks. Hence, if you are a kind of person that is more comfortable with those risks, then you'll find, probably, that entrepreneurs are the major risk takers. Thus, you are destined to be an employer than an employee, who knows how to manage risks well. Hence, employers are not just blindly jumping into a risky situation, they accept risk, but they also know how to ensure that the rest of their life is more stable, that's where your trouble comes sometimes. Consequently, they can continue doing what they do, which is something that excites about them.

In conclusion, the personality building is a very important part of the process. It's not just the result of the personality in the fact sheet that you build, but it's catalyzing yourself to really start to think, what my personality is and everything you do have to be aligned with it.

Remember, we discuss this age old adage before? I hope you do and I kept it for latter to talk about because it is actually a later stage that you become a jack of all trades where there is no point discussing it at the beginning. The adage warns about people who can be called generalist, where Chinese say, "Equipped with Knives all over, yet none is sharp". Instead, I suggested you to be a master of many to be unique and standalone from the crowd. If you consider most of the impactful and legends in the modern day or in old world are generalists including Galileo, Aristotle to Charles Darwin, Leonardo Da Vinci, Thomas Edison to modern day Steve Jobs, Elon Musk or Warren Buffett, Larry Page, and Jeff Bezos. Thus, you can say all of them are Jack of all trades or in other words as to the modern day terminology, they all are polymaths.

Anyway, why do we talk about all of them? I told you, when you become a jack of all trades you should start your own because there will be so many enemies around you more than ever. Hence, your life will be utmost difficult in an organization, rather than enjoying your skills. However, throughout all these pages, I was trying to tell you to become a jack of all trades and master of many instead of been master of none which is somewhat beyond generalist. Thus, a polymath will be the most relevant term which means a person who knows a lot about a lot of subjects. In other words, when a person's knowledge covers many diverse areas he or she is become a polymath which is the real technical phenomena behind it.

However, I'm not trying to teach you 'How to become a polymath' since you can find hell lots of reading and instruction on internet as usual. We already discussed how you can improve your subject knowledge and expanding the number of subjects' alternative to your main function. Hence, all these topics points toward one direction, where you need to become a one of the most wanted people in the organization which you can't achieve in a single night. The well-rounded is another similar term that you can use for the same polymath, i.e. you can explain someone as a quality assurance manager, who is also a system designer with the ability of creating fully equipped production facility designs while being a dancer and a writer with the ability of selling ice to Eskimos in Arctic. In other words people who can bring best across the several fields to be more effective in their respective field.

If you are planning to become an expert in a single field you may need around 10,000 hours of deliberate practice to beat the competition. However, modern day polymaths are acting against the general advice of being expert in a single field by building different combinations of skillset and knowledge across diversified fields. Then integrate these skillsets to create breakthrough ideas or even brand new fields and industries where there is a blue ocean with very little competition. This is one of another reasons to jump-ship, because it gives you the ability of learning across different positions or organizations in a diversified functions. Hence, you will be able to create difference among competitors while being a game changer and a survivor in any kind of storm.

Listen more, Talk less

As we already discussed the "survival of the fittest", and the evolution theory of Charles Darwin, I would like to further explain some of his abilities of applications across diverse fields. If you read the "**Where Good Ideas Come From**", a book published by Steven Johnson in 2010 where his character has been explained in following manner. Darwin had "to solve the mystery, he had to think like a naturalist, a marine biologist and a geologist all at once. He had to understand the life cycle of coral colonies and observe the tiny evidence of organic sculpture on the rocks of the Keeling Islands; he had to think on the immense time scales of volcanic mountains rising and falling into the sea. To understand the idea in its full complexity required a kind of probing intelligence, willing to think across those different disciplines and scales". So you can understand how polymath's life can be complex as well as required skills to standalone.

According to Michael Simmons article "people who have too many interests are more likely to be successful according to research", who explicitly explains that, there are two ways of becoming extraordinary in your carrier. That are; becoming the best at one specific filed of yours or becoming very good (top 25%) at two or more things which will give you a leapfrog value to your future. However, becoming the best in a single field is a very difficult task. On the other hand, everyone has at least few areas of inborn advantages where they can create some difference by training themselves to become very good at those fields while achieving good reputation. In such cases, if you connect these diverse fields across your work opportunities while creating unique results that may improve your survival. Because it is the most important part of lots of job descriptions where many people have limited success or skills across diverse fields, since most creative breakthroughs come via making atypical combinations of skills. On contrary, it is easier to learn few subjects up to a competent level rather than becoming a subject expert. It is not a very difficult task since, current learning environment in digital age offers you several different tool sets to master whole new subject without much efforts which is already discussed before.

Because quality of learning is improving in every domain due to the systematic updating and scientific explorations of existing old fallacious understandings into new robust information. Nonetheless, existence of web has created opportunities for free or affordable material from world top experts in every domain of study with thousands of freely available courses or coaching sessions. Thus, you need to invest on yourself to make sure that you learn the best up-to-date tactics in your respective filed. On contrary, current explosion of knowledge has also created extreme difficulties of being an expert due to the speed of explosion where nobody will be able to grab all of them in such a short period. Henceforth, it has further expanded the option of being a polymath through exploring quickly atypical combination of fields or skills rather than becoming a subject expert. Therefore, you must be able to combine your newly acquired skillset with old ones in the industry or field which will eventually generate far better results than usual in most cases. As your number of new skillsets are increased, the possible combinations are increased exponentially with cross combination of different fields together. In fact, practical application will sharpen potential skills while creating an environment for every new breakthrough with potential for exponentially more breakthroughs, whereas every new chunk of knowledge can be combined with every other chunk theoretically.

According to Charles Darwin "It is not the strongest or the most intelligent who will survive but those who can best manage change" or the highly adaptable because we can't see through time. Hence, we need to adapt to the change so quickly or otherwise our survival is lost. That's why you need to manage yourself to become a jack of all trades, while mastering across several fields rather than becoming a subject expert of one domain. I hope the term polymath is more meaningful and convenient than jack of all trades. Naturally, once you become a polymath you can combine them across diverse fields while mastering the unique fields before others where you will stand out the competition in modern corporate world.

The new skills you gain will create breakthrough innovations to solve complex problems which will have a great impact. Yet, others who fail to synthesize their knowledge into value, flounder in their career even though they may have comprehensive knowledge, without a real impact. Most of the time, specialist has the risk of getting trapped into their own success. Because, they have built highly paid narrowed skillsets with fragile future, as their respected professions disappear or revolved it will be very difficult for them to switch without starting over, where polymaths are normally anti-fragile.

As a rule of thumb, you will not be able to find head or tail at the beginning although you want to become a polymath. There are diverse fields of opportunities, but you might not know what the best is for you. Hence, I recommend you to read Michel Simmons article which will give you much more insights of the subject. You also can follow his online courses or free email course or mini course. Nonetheless, there are millions of data on the net about being polymath where you only need time and interest. If you keep trying, it will definitely make you a polymath which you don't need to be inherited, that you can easily cultivate into your corporate carrier.

In addition, as Elle Antonia Young explains in the **Lifeheck** blog under "How to become a modern day polymath", you can find some of the very easiest steps towards the objective. As it suggests, be curious and open to learning, cultivate multiple passions and interests, don't worry about being perfect, reject gate keepers and set realistic goals and follow through. I hope these five simple steps may help you to go through it, but you need to research into the areas and competencies before you start making your multiple skillsets.

$\mathcal{N}$ow let's see some of the explored and unexplored lessons for you to succeed in any job, because it is important to know the grounds better. We were discussing different topics with many stories, but I usually don't want to make this book to be very long since today's world is too busy for it. On the other hand, you don't have that much of time to read all your life.

Sometime it is better to learn before you do the mistake, because you at least know that you are going to be in trouble if you know it beforehand. Therefore, eventually your mind and body use to avoid risks where it use to find short cuts. Thus, it is very important that you read whatever good material you got and keep things in mind. Hence, this is going to be the last chapter we walk across together. Since I want to conclude this book with some good ending for you to keep them in memory; I have added many taglines we kept here and there at the end. As a matter of fact, you will forget all what I said within weeks, but those old adages or saying will be remembered for a long time. Indeed, you might remember them before you do some mistakes and start to think twice before you do it. Actually, there is nothing new but these little ideas can create a great person around you if you follow the rules, because they are practically proven.

> ### Trust everyone, but never trust the devil inside them

You came across this, do you remember? How many girlfriends or boyfriends of yours have break the trust? How many times you break their trust more importantly? I hope we all *have break trust of others once in a way, whatever promises we gave to them. Hence, there is no point too much trusting other people, I usually don't even trust my parents much more than usual, even though they are the only people we can really trust at least in life, not even your brother or sister, or wife or husband. I hope they are the most untrustworthy people around anybody, if you only consider lying as a matter of fact. How many times we have lied to them to keep our relationship or trust long-lasting? If you haven't lied to your partner once in a while, your present relationship is no more, just imagine for an example last month; how many lies you have use to save your ass. I hope there may be one or two percentage of people don't fall in to this category and I'm not talking about those uncommon people.*

To be honest, we all lie others in order to keep our relationships intact or to hide our real faces most of the time. But we always say we trust each other and trust is the most important bond between us. So trust every one, it is good a thing, but always remember, he might have to lie for some unforeseen reason or to save his some other fabrication which has been already told. Thus, we don't know what to trust or what is not to trust. Consequently, you can trust everything other person say or do and you can keep it until he is get caught, but you should not trust what he will do next based on what he said.

Every person has several faces in their lives, so they usually show you one face while he show another face to someone else. He might be very honorable person, but if he is in great trouble where he may find that it is easy to put his troubles on your name and safeguard himself. Do you think if such an option is available, he might not consider it, no my friend, he will definitely consider it, whether he take that option or not. That's the devil I'm talking about, even if you are not doing anything wrong, you still might be thinking of options you've got which is the problem. If a person came across the prisoner's dilemma, he might take the option to save himself than to think about the other. Thus, it is always safe to trust every one and not to trust their inner devil that we don't know much about and don't take granted for whatever person says. Do not expect too much from anybody which is much safer and a best option.

Show Respect to others then only you will be respected

We do believe that we need to be respected, don't we? Yes we deserve for it, but if you want to be respected the most important thing is that you need to respect the others, because nobody will respect you unless otherwise you don't respect them. As we all know the old adage, "what we harvest is what we sow". Thus, it is you who should start respecting others, which has no limitations or boundaries once you start to respect others. Because, you are not expecting anything but respecting others, their culture, religion, beliefs, or anything they value as something important to them, if you want to get respected. Let's say for an example that you start to call people with Miss/Mrs. or Mr.; from the very first moment you meet someone to talk to. Instantly you will see that other person also will start calling you the same way, or whatever you are worthy of. If you continue to practice this on all the time everyone will also call you the same way that you talk to them, since people love to be respected. When you offer the respect to the other people, they feel ashamed or guilty if they don't respect you in the same way. It is one of the easiest things to practice since everyone expecting it from you, where it is very easy tool to be polite and disciplined too.

Show off a little bit- Don't let yourself go unnoticed

Do you think that you should go completely unnoticed? No it is not! I think it is very important to make sure that you are well noticed in the event of any important event or work related happening in your work environment, which we discussed briefly before. That's important to show off sometimes what really you are, but don't show everything what you got or things that you don't have. Because in working environments as we already discussed, lots of executives get the credit because they have subordinates who really owns the innovation or improvement, but his boss get credited for what he has found. This usually happens because lots of high rankers do not own innovative minds or time to think.

Fortunately, they have a large crews, where they sometimes come up with lots of new ideas. Fortunate for them, most of the time subordinate got a new idea, their boss get credited while they go unnoticed because they never try to make little bit of show off themselves before releasing such information. It is not bad to tell the boss, but it will be much better if you can do the same explanation when the CEO or GM or even owner is at your doorstep for something else or may be in a meeting, where you can explain the matter rather than directly exposing to your boss. Sometimes companies setup rewards for any improvement idea or some new cost cutting initiative to improve the bottom up information as well as to reward rightful owners of innovations. But it is not everywhere and most of the time real inventors go unnoticed while someone else get the credit.

On the other hand, if you are good at something whether your core competency or something else you need to show up little bit that who you are and what really your competencies are when you get the right opportunity as we already discussed.

Nonetheless, even after you were gone, people will remember for what you are whether you are good or bad. We insist that, it is always good to be a nice person with many talent as well as showing off little bit that what you really are. If you are good at fighting, and if everyone knows that you can fight but you usually not a hot guy. I hope people will understand the danger of challenging you, which will give an advantage of very few people try to mess up with you in that way. However, if no one knows that you are a good fighter, sometimes you get challenges even from the very innocent people you never expect to believe.

Tell the time by looking at the other person's watch

He will tell you the time, by looking at your own watch; which is the practical definition of a consultant, because he don't have any problems or answers when he visit any client. Thus, client have so much of problems and answers where consultant's job is to find him the right answers from all the answers he already know. However, if you want to understand that, you should wear his shoes and look at from his perspectives to understand real situation he is in; (see things from the other person's point of view to see what he has seen). Then you might need to talk to the right person in his subordinate team to find out the real issue as well as the best possible answer. Sometimes the reality is that, he might not listening to his subordinates. Usually he may try to find his own solution or he might not value one of his grass rooter's idea which might have sorted out the problem very long time ago if he has better ears. Thus, if you do not understand the person in front of you or did not look at from his point of view of the problem, you might not find the solution.

As a little example, I use to write business proposals for business clients, who needs to find financing for their projects. Recently, I wrote a proposal which worth several millions that I finished within 3 days and send him to tell me what need to be changed or to see if it was the right idea that he bears in mind. I only sat with him about 3 hours and let him talk about many things related to his business idea. I had to ask several questions while disturbing him. I also did a complete study of his business operation for another hour through a plant work through audit. After I sent him the draft he told me that, there were only very few minor corrections and he even can write this because he knows everything. So I said to him that yes because it is your idea and you wanted it on the paper to get a loan from the bank, and you didn't asked me to write down your biography. I charged him half a million to write this where he was bargaining terribly. However at the end, most importantly he also said this. "I feel like I can do it, because I know all these things, but if I had do that, I never accomplish this because it is not my skill and I don't know head or tail of the bank requirements or the way I need to present it. So you purified my idea, of course you are liable to get paid". Hence, you may understand the idea, you need to look from others eyes, but you need to evaluate form you mind and apply it for the right cause to get better results.

Once you collect enough experiences and if you are an expert of your subject, you may be able to become a consultant. However, if *you are not a good listener as well as if you can't make people talking to you, it is not a very great position to practice. Because, you need to find a way to make sure people have little trust on you to talk. Then they will tell about themselves as well as what they really experienced, without which you will not be able to find out right solutions for them. Be a great listener, full triggers where you can make people talking, which is very important, because if you find someone very less talking, few things you can guess. Number one, he don't like you or the subject you are trying to discuss with or he may be hiding something. Easy guess isn't it?*

I hope some of the topics we explored bit deeply in some occasions, but now it is the time to summarize all of them and to finally find your stand inside any company. The following topics are a summery one of my intern gave to me before she ended up her training when I asked her what you learn from your training before she quit. I asked her to jot down what you have learned from me while she was under my department. She was the one that asked me to write a book on these things that I sometimes explained to them about the corporate world and how you need to survive in the work place. Actually they follow most of them and became necessary people than permanent employees in the company. That was the point I through to write these little stories into a book which we already came across some of those stories before.

As a summary of what we discussed before I'm adding this as my final sentences or as the take away list of the book. Most of these taglines are not mine, they are there from a prehistoric time. Some of them are idioms, some of them are I found here and there, some are my own. Whoever said or owned them, I learned so much life lessons from them, may be before I know them or may be after I know them. As we always say no body's perfect, where you need to learn from your mistakes. Most of the things I learned, I really learned from my mistakes and by observing them. If you look at things you will learn nothing, so just try to observe things and try to remember things which will give you many stories about the same thing you never know before.

The Recap for You

Be a good example to others.

Be a happy employee.

Be nice and pleasant, do not be high and mighty.

Be open-minded.

Be positive.

Be punctual.

Be quick and accurate.

Be smart. Once in a while; dodge the ball and let it pass.

Be techno-economical.

Be trustworthy.

Before the end of the day; clean the work lot on your table.

Behave, be disciplined.

Bend the rules.

Better late than never.

Beware from gossip.

Boss is Boss - He is always right - He is an idiot.

Choose a job you love, and you will never have to work a day in your life.

Choose positive living over negative mind.

Do it right even when no one is looking.

Do not overdo.

Do not repeat the same mistake twice.

Do not take in and take out personal problems to work.

Do not waste a mili-second.

Do what you say, Say what you do, and Write what you do.

Don't find fault, find a remedy.

Don't let other's voice drown yours.

Don't watch, Observe.

Evaluate your progress.

Experience, position, & salary

Focus, focus, focus

Follow your intuition.

Get in line with the culture.

Give your best and great will be your reward.

Have a notebook and pen in your pocket always - Jot down everything important.

Have a plan - day, monthly, yearly.

Have background knowledge.

If you don't have good company, better be alone and silent.

It is better to aim at perfection and miss it than to aim at imperfection and hit it.

Keep your Friends close, Enemies closer.

Know your enemy.

Lay a firm foundation with the bricks others throw at you.

Listen more, Talk less.

Listen to everyone; Solutions arise even from the low level workers.

Maintain a "to do list"

Maintain your status.

Make an entrance - Make a difference.

Minimize errors; do not give others' the satisfaction of criticizing you.

More work more problems- No work no problems.

Never say Never.

Nobody is perfect, No system is perfect, No company is perfect.

Obey rules.

Prevention is better than cure.

Show off a little bit, don't let yourself go unnoticed.

Show Respect to others then only you will be respected

Start small and dream big.

Stay within your limit.

Take the experience first; the money will follow you later.

Tell the time by looking at the other person's watch

Think before Act.

Think before Talk.

Think out of box.

Too much of anything is not too good.

Trust everyone, but never trust the devil inside them

Wait for the right time to make the move

Watch and learn.

When you go to work, don't leave your heart at home.

Who is your customer?

Work Hard, Work Smart.

You need to follow, in order to lead

Bold is Beautiful

www.ingramcontent.com/pod-product-compliance
Lightning Source LLC
Chambersburg PA
CBHW070400200326
41518CB00011B/1994